History of the
Spirit Lake Massacre
and Captivity of
Miss Abbie Gardner

MRS. ABBIE GARDNER-SHARP

History of the Spirit Lake Massacre and Captivity of Miss Abbie Gardner

The Raid of the Santee Sioux Against the
Iowa Frontier Settlements, 1857

Mrs. Abbie Gardner-Sharp

LEONAUR

History of the Spirit Lake Massacre and Captivity of Miss Abbie Gardner
The Raid of the Santee Sioux Against the Iowa Frontier Settlements, 1857
by Mrs. Abbie Gardner-Sharp

First published under the title
History of the Spirit Lake Massacre and Captivity of Miss Abbie Gardner

Leonaur is an imprint of Oakpast Ltd

Copyright in this form © 2011 Oakpast Ltd

ISBN: 978-0-85706-637-4 (hardcover)
ISBN: 978-0-85706-638-1 (softcover)

http://www.leonaur.com

Publisher's Notes

The opinions of the authors represent a view of events in which she
was a participant related from her own perspective,
as such the text is relevant as an historical document.

The views expressed in this book are not necessarily
those of the publisher.

Contents

Preface

It was with a great degree of embarrassment that I assented to the various invitations extended to me, to place upon record the recollections of my youth, and group the incidents for a history of that tragic event, generally known as the "Spirit Lake Massacre," which so far had gone unwritten, and, no progress made in that direction.

Believing that a local history of this lovely lake region is demanded, on account of its becoming the favourite summer resort in the great northwest; and because the awful events of the massacre transpired here, I have, amid physical ills which have disqualified me for the active pursuits of life, devoted two years of painful labour to indicting the bitter reminiscences, and gathering the facts, dates, and events recorded in this volume.

In doing so I hope to benefit myself, pay a lasting tribute to the memory of those whose lives were consecrated to civilization, and save from oblivion the historical matter within these pages.

Being fully conscious of my inability to execute, to the satisfaction of the public, a task so responsible, I would have been glad, for the sake of history, to impart my knowledge of the bloody drama to one whose gifted pen would have been more worthy of the subject; but, by sad misfortune—which has followed my captivity—the duty has fallen upon me.

Thus, I have undertaken the task, relying confidently upon the generous reader for a justification of the motives by which I was actuated; relying upon the maxim that *truth is mighty, and will prevail*, without the glitter of rhetoric.

Errors, in some particulars may be found; but, in view of the pains and labour taken to guard against them, it is believed they are few and unimportant.

The articles found within, which are not original, are credited to their respective authors, most of whom were active participators in the transactions of which they write.

I am greatly indebted to friends, who have kindly aided me, and furnished me every facility in their power, by which the history should lack nothing of completeness. Without the assistance of the persons referred to, this book would not, at this time, be presented to the public.

I now commit my work to the public, trusting the labour expended upon it will not be lost.

Abbie Gardner-Sharp.

May 12 1885.

CHAPTER 1

Rowland Gardner

Rowland Gardner was born in the year 1815, in New Haven, Connecticut. On the bank of a rapid stream nearby, stood a factory for the manufacture of combs. Employed there, he spent several years of his youth. Tiring of the daily routine of factory life, he started in quest of a new home: and in early manhood located in the beautiful and fertile plateau lying between the smiling waters of the "Twin Lakes," Seneca and Cayuga, in Seneca County, in the grand old state of New York. With all its fine mountain scenery, and sparkling rivulets, the state contains few more romantic spots than this one at "Twin Lakes."

At this place, on the 22nd day of March, 1836, he was united in marriage with Frances M. Smith, of a devoted Christian family. As time passed, their home was made happy by the advent of four children, Mary M., Eliza M., Abigail, and Rowland, youngest child and only son.

Abigail, youngest girl and writer of this history, was born in 1843. While yet a child and earlier than I can remember, we moved to Greenwood, Steuben county, in western New York. Here strolling with my sisters, by Canisteo's rippling waters, climbing the rugged slope of the towering hills, or listening to the buzz of the great saw in fathers saw mill, in sportive joy I whiled away some of the pleasantest hours of my life; and it is with fond recollection that I wander back in memory to those delightful scenes of childhood,—to joys which were so complete in the happy days at Greenwood.

My first school days, too, were passed at that place, and pleasant memories are awakened by thoughts of my teachers, Lydia Davis and Sarah Starr. My parents were members of the Methodist Episcopal Church, and consistent Christians. During their stay in New York they enjoyed church privileges, which they were deprived of ever after, in life. Father was also a strict temperance man, never using either spirituous liquors or tobacco in any form, and it was his constant endeavour to instil into the minds of his children principles of temperance and virtue. In the year 1850, he purchased a saw mill in the village of Rexville, a few miles from Greenwood, and again the family were called upon to pass through the vicissitudes of establishing another home.

Oh, that he might have been content with a well earned promise of success! Instead of being laid low in an unknown grave in the western wilderness, he might have amassed a fortune, and had a long and happy life, in a peaceful, quiet home. The war-whoop of the Indian would never have echoed through his dwelling; the tomahawk and scalping-knife never would have horrified his children; nor his family have been brought to an untimely end. And the writer of these pages would never have been called upon to record such sad events.

But, like many others, my father was confident that greater success awaited him. His ambition was like that of thousands of others, who seem to think that because it is best for some to go west, it is best for each one to go farthest west of all. Thus the race is kept up. We chase the setting sun; and, like the boy in pursuit of the rainbow, we hope to find the pot of gold just beyond.

While the family resided at Rexville, the eldest daughter, Mary, was married to Mr. Harvey Luce, of Huron County, Ohio. Without dwelling upon this to us very interesting event, the counsels of parents, and congratulations of friends, we will briefly say: that she (whom we will in future call Mrs. Luce) bade *adieu* to her girlhood home; to parents, sisters, and brother, and departed with her husband, to enter upon new scenes and associations in Ohio.

In the summer of 1853, two years later, father and mother, with their three remaining children, bade farewell forever to relatives and neighbours; to the pine-clad hills of New York; to the rushing of the waterfall; with all the familiar associations clustering about them; all to be exchanged for the broad, rich prairies of the "far west," and the exciting, adventurous life of the pioneer. The journey was performed in the old fashioned way, with horses and wagons. During the journey the nights were spent at hotels, or "inns," as they were then more commonly called.

Jolly times we children had! every day bringing its store of novelties, as our course led us through villages; by fields of waving grain or grassy meadows; over beautiful streams, and through shady woodlands.

But, best of all, we were going to see sister Mary, and (for the first time) her prattling little "blue-eyed baby boy." At Norwalk, Ohio, we were joined by Mr. and Mrs. Luce, and continued our journey to the north-western part of the state, where father took a con- tract of grading on the "Lake Shore and Michigan Southern Railroad." This was followed into Indiana, where new contracts were made, rendering a handsome profit.

During our short sojourn in these two localities, sister Eliza and myself continued our studies in school. Realizing the worth of a thorough education, it was father's purpose to give us every advantage he could. My school days, however, were over when I was less than fourteen years of age; ended by circumstances which will be only too evident as the reader progresses.

Father was an energetic, wide-awake man—a true type of the pioneer—and when he left the state of New York it was his settled intention to go west of the Mississippi, and make his home on the far-famed prairies of Iowa. Accordingly in the fall of 1854, our family, in company with Mr. and Mrs. Luce and one child, turned our backs upon civilization, its comforts and refinements, to take up again the line of march. Our route led through the northern part of Illinois. At the city of Joliet we made a short halt. Here a little incident occurred which gave me a foretaste of some of the anguish that awaited me. Having ascertained the road which we should take, father gave the proper instructions to mother (who was driving our team), telling her to drive on; that he would buy some bread for supper, and soon overtake us.

It was just dusk as we drove outside the city limits, expecting every minute to be rejoined by the head of our party. But we had taken the wrong street, and of course no father appeared. Mr. Luce went back to the city in search of him, but returned alone. Mother sought no shelter that night but the cover of the wagon, and there kept a light burning until daylight. In sleepless suspense she passed the lonely night, fearing that some calamity had befallen him. After crying awhile, brother and I, childlike, drowned our trouble in sleep until morning.

Father having taken the right road, of course, could get no trace of us, as the emigrants had been seen by no one. At length, being convinced that we had strayed, he sought shelter in a farmhouse, where he passed a sleepless night. Early next morning he started out in search of the lost emigrants. At the same time Mr. Luce, with several other men, went on horseback after the lost man. In a few hours the lost were found, and we resumed our journey.

We crossed the "Father of waters" at Rock Island, entered the state of Iowa at Davenport, and continued our journey to the northwest. The wide-spreading prairies were indeed a grand sight to those who had lived only among the thickly wooded hills of the eastern states. As we advanced, the settlements became more scattered; the villages smaller, and more remote from each other. Some days passed without even a sight of a town. Then for the first time I began to realize whither we were going; and that if the journey continued a few days longer we should indeed find the great wild country for which we were headed.

Crossing the Cedar River at Janesville, we followed the valley of the Shell Rock until we came to the village bearing its name. We were only one hundred miles west of the Mississippi, but the chilly winds of October warned us of the approach of winter, and it was decided to remain at Shell Rock until spring, or until the selection of lands on which to settle

At present writing this is a thrifty town of over one thousand inhabitants; but when we entered the place there were no churches, no schoolhouses, not even a store; the settlers being compelled to go to Janesville for supplies. The settlement was then all on the east side of the river. Some members of the families with whom we became acquainted that winter are still residents there. Among them may be mentioned Hiram Ross and J. L. Stewart.

As there were no churches, religious services were held in the private houses. The winter passed pleasantly, and in early spring father started on a prospecting tour. When he returned we were again called upon to part with our acquaintances and go out into the unknown.

In all these different homes my sister Eliza and myself—though only a child—had made many friends among our schoolmates from whom we regretted to part. The oft repeated "goodbyes," and promises "never to forget each other," still linger in my memory, and it is with feelings of tenderness that I make mention of my childhood friends. As the autumn leaves, when once broken from the parent stem, are whirled away by every breeze, so father found it easy, when once he had begun to move, to pull up stakes again and seek his fortune still further west.

Thus in March, 1855, we were again on the move. Our course still led up the Shell Rock valley to where the town of Nora Springs now stands, thence west to Mason City, which consisted of one store and two or three other buildings; from here to Clear Lake—ten miles distant—the place of our destination.

My father was an ardent lover of nature, especially enjoying that indescribable charm which water lends to a landscape; so we were not surprised at his selection of a farm in the vicinity of such attractions as those at Clear Lake.

CHAPTER 2

Clear Lake

Clear Lake today, (as at time of first publication), is one of the popular summer resorts of the northwest. Thousands of people gather here every summer. Aside from the attractions which nature offers to pleasure seekers, the Methodist conferences of northern Iowa have here established permanent camp-meeting grounds. They secure the best talent of the country to conduct religious services, and also offer superior advantages to lovers of music, temperance, etc. In July, 1851—four years before our coming there—Joseph Hewitt and James Dickerson, with their families, made the first settlement at the lake. These two families enjoyed the wild romance of a home at Clear Lake two years before they were joined by other settlers.

You, my reader, who live in city or town, enjoying your churches, schools, railroads, telephones, and all the conveniences of modern civilization, unless you have been a pioneer, little know what it is to live as these good people did, sixty-five miles from their nearest neighbour.

For the benefit of any who may want to know the locality of our home at Clear Lake, I will say, the farm is now traversed by the Chicago, Milwaukee & St. Paul Railroad, and owned by Mr. Elon Tuttle. A nicer place is hard to find in Cerro Gordo county. During the time we resided at the lake my sister Eliza was engaged in teaching school in one of the two rooms of Mr. Hewitt's log house. The average attendance was seventeen; for which she received one dollar per month for each pupil, and board. This was the first school ever taught in that county. The distance being too great for me to attend, as well as for a son of Mr. Dickerson, he and father engaged Mrs. Styles to instruct us. We pursued our studies in her home; while she attended to her household duties, stopping to hear us recite. Interesting and lively recitations they were; and many merry hours we passed in childish sport, upon the premises of Mr. Styles.

Messrs. Hewitt and Dickerson had experienced some trouble with the Sioux Indians; which was brought about by the vicious Sioux killing a young Winnebago. Not content with killing him, they severed his head from his body and carried it to their camp.

Before locating at Clear Lake, Mr. Hewitt had (at one time) been a trader with the Winnebagoes in the northeast part of the state. Upon learning that their old friend Hewitt was at the lake several families of them came and pitched their *teepes* around his house. Ever on friendly terms, they came and went without giving the least trouble to the settlers.

The Sioux—on the contrary—were always a terror to the whites. They were cunning, treacherous, and bloodthirsty, and the most dreaded tribe in the west. Roving bands of this hostile tribe occasionally made their appearance at the lake feigning at first to be friendly with both the whites and Winnebagoes, frequently smoking the pipe of peace with the latter. To-shan-e-ga, one of the Winnebagoes, however, expressed to the settlers his suspicions of the evil intentions of the Sioux. As the sequel will prove, his suspicion was well founded; for it was not long until a couple of Sioux secreted themselves in a thicket of willows, by the roadside, and shot a Winnebago boy about sixteen years old, while he was out hunting for Mr. Hewitt's cows. Being only few in number the Winnebagoes became greatly alarmed at this evidence of hostility, and immediately sought the residence of their friend, Mr. Hewitt, and begged of him to help them out of the country; as they feared the enemy would return in greater numbers on the following day and murder them all. Accordingly, they were loaded into a covered wagon, and (with Mr. Hewitt's hired man for driver) were conveyed beyond the reach of their enemy; and so returned to their own hunting ground in safety.

At this time Mr. Dickerson lived on the prairie about one mile east of the lake. A few days after the occurrence above related, the men perceived approaching, over the prairie, within a quarter of a mile of the house, some five hundred Sioux warriors, all armed with rifles. As these cruel savages marched toward the house, their guns glistening in the noon-day sun, it made our brave frontiersmen feel how utterly they were at their mercy, had they chosen to take advantage of them.

Mr. Hewitt fastened a white cloth to a pole, and went forward with the "flag of truce" to meet them, determined, if possible, to learn their intentions, and avert trouble. The Indians halted a short distance from

15

the house, and the chief advanced to meet him. It was learned that they intended to kill the Winnebagoes, and believing that they were concealed about the premises of the whites, they had come to search them out. Mr. Hewitt told them the Winnebagoes had left the country. But the wily Sioux believed this merely a trick to deceive them, and would not give up their intention to search the house.

To satisfy them Mr. Hewitt told them, if they would leave their guns on the prairie, where they were, he and Mr. Dickerson would carry all their weapons out of the house, and they might make the search. To this the chief agreed, and nineteen warriors were detailed for this purpose. They looked in every nook and corner, from the flour barrel to the attic, before being convinced that the Winnebagoes had escaped. Finally, being satisfied, they filed out of the house, and as they collected in the yard each warrior drew from under his blanket a loaded revolver; waving them in the air, they gave the settlers to understand that had they found their prey they too would have shared death at the hands of a relentless foe.

By a treaty between the government and the Indians, some time previous, this part of the country was declared neutral ground. It is readily seen how little respect this latter party had for the treaty; having first murdered an inoffensive boy, returned in force to kill the remainder of the band, that had not even resented the outrage, as well as any whites who might be found befriending them. The band soon returned to their own hunting ground, greatly to the relief of the two families. To this and other adventures with the Indians—when related to our family by those who participated in them—I listened with thrilling interest. Having never yet seen any of the frightful beings, I began in imagination to picture them, and dread their appearance, as they were now likely to be seen any day. I could think of nothing so dreadful as the war-painted faces of the red-skins.

I had listened to the stories of their cruel deeds, when seated by mother's side, in our far away home in New York. Now, living in an Indian region, I felt that all I had ever imagined might become real.

CHAPTER 3

Grindstone War

We had resided at Clear Lake several months before an Indian made his appearance. In the month of June a large number of them came and encamped about seven miles north of the lake on Lime Creek. As is their custom, when in the vicinity of the whites, a lot of them went through the settlement on a begging expedition. It is impossible to express my abhorrence for those repulsive and ferocious looking beings, as they entered our house and began at once to ask for something to eat; nor did they ask for victuals alone, but whatever they thought serviceable, or what pleased their fancy, they persistently demanded, all the while jabbering their Indian jargon. To get rid of them as soon as possible they were fed bountifully, and what they asked for was given them, if it could be spared.

While they were ransacking the house and premises of Mr. Dickerson that day an incident occurred that created a great excitement among the settlers, and finds a place in the annals of that time under the title of the "Grindstone War." It led to the abandonment, for a time, of nearly all that portion of the frontier, and spread alarm far into the settlements.

The liberal treatment they received did not satisfy them. A handsome rooster that was strutting about at the head of Mr. Dickerson's thrifty flock of fowls attracted the attention of an impertinent young redskin, who commenced chasing it about the yard, while his brawny comrades encouraged him with shouts of laughter. Mr. Dickerson called to him to desist, and plainly showed his disapprobation. The Indian, however, killed the chicken, and in the chase knocked over the grindstone, breaking it in pieces. He then seized the largest piece and started off with it.

By this time Mr. Dickerson was following him with a club, but at the entreaties of his wife and Mrs. Marcus Tuttle he threw down the weapon, fearing that the Indians might become exasperated and kill them all on the spot. He, however, jerked the grindstone away, and sent the Indian sprawling on the ground. The latter jumped up, grabbed his gun, cocked it, and threatened to shoot, whereupon Mr. Dickerson seized a piece of the stone and knocked him down, where he lay several minutes. The Indians them demanded that Mr. Dickerson pay the wounded Indian one hundred dollars, or give him a horse. Mr. Dickerson refused to do either. His wife, fearing the consequences, begged him to comply with their demands. As he offered no reconciliation, Mrs. Dickerson gave them what, money she had in the house (five or six dollars), some bed-quilts, and several other articles of less value. This pacified the injured Indian, and they all left the premises without further trouble.

The news of this little incident soon spread over the entire settlement. The whites apprehended that danger was in store for them; that the Indians would send for re-enforcements, and come upon them and massacre the whole settlement. They were well aware of the treachery and craftiness of the Sioux. The next morning all the men around the lake, with a number from Mason City, assembled and organized under the leadership of John Long, of Mason City. The little band of about twenty-five men, well armed and mounted, started out resolved to clear the country of the troublesome invaders.

All the men being now away from home the terrible situation in which the families were placed can only be imagined. In some cases several women gathered in the house of one of the number, hoping thus for greater safety, while others barricaded the doors of their cabins, and waited there alone the result of the anticipated conflict. Still others left their houses and sought safety by hiding in the tall grass. All expected, every moment, to hear the sounds of the battle, where father and son would join in the deadly conflict, and probably fall victims to the sure aim of the Indian's rifle. The result being uncertain, the suspense was terrible. Minutes seemed like hours and hours like days to those helpless women and children, while that little band of brave men were risking their lives for the peace and safety of those dependent upon them.

My mother, whose fears were almost beyond her control, suggested that we leave our cabin and hide in the tall thick grass that grew along the creek, just back of the barn, hoping the Indians—if victorious— would not look for us there. We all knew that if the Indians were the victors we would have to share the fate of our defenders.

Mrs. Luce had more courage than mother, or else felt more confidence in the power of our little army, for she maintained that it would be of no use to run, and she proposed to stand her ground, at least until after dinner, for if she was to be killed she did not want to die hungry.

But how fared the little company of improvised soldiers as they marched toward the camp of the Sioux? Coming in sight of the camp they soon perceived that the savages were aware of their approach, as they were in great commotion, and soon formed themselves into line of battle.

In honour to the little band of white men it must be said not one of them faltered. Although the enemy outnumbered them greatly, they pressed gallantly forward, determined to repel the insolent invaders, or die in the attempt.

The Indians awaited the onset until they were almost within gunshot, when the chief advanced with a flag of truce in one hand and a great pipe in the other. He stopped a short distance from the whites (who also halted), and set his flagstaff in the ground, indicating that he desired a *parley*. Captain Long advanced. The chief told him that his people did not want any trouble with the white settlers.

To this the captain replied that the settlers had always fed them, and treated them kindly, although the Indians had frequently been guilty of bad conduct toward them, and now they were determined to endure their insolence no longer. He then demanded that the money and articles given by Mrs. Dickerson to the Indian who had caused the trouble should be refunded, and that the band should forthwith leave that part of the country. The money and other articles were brought out, and the other stipulations agreed to. The old chief then desired that the pipe of peace should be smoked between himself and the whole company of soldiers. The pipe being lighted the chief shook hands with the captain and handed him the pipe. He took a single whiff and returned it to the chief, who also took a single whiff. This ceremony was repeated until all the men had shaken hands and smoked with the old Indian. This ended the ceremony of a treaty of peace, and the chief promised to lead his warriors away before the setting of another sun.

The settlers manifested their confidence by returning to their homes, where they were gladly hailed by the women and children, who had for hours been suffering the keenest pangs of suspense.

The next morning early a man went out to see if the Indians had left their camp. Not one was to be seen. Such was the beginning and happy ending of the once famous "Grindstone War," without shedding of other blood than that of James Dickerson's old rooster, whose lustrous feathers and lordly strut were the innocent cause of the outbreak. From that day to this the Sioux have never crossed the boundary of Cerro Gordo County.

But the treaty so unexpectedly made did not allay the fears of the settlers. They could not repose confidence in the promises of the Sioux, whom they knew to be utterly regardless of the rights of the white man. It was believed the Indians had only gone to gain numbers, or to wait till the settlers were off their guard, when they would return and massacre them all. Hence for several days a watch was kept constantly, but as no Sioux appeared the conviction that danger no longer existed gradually gained ground until a feeling of safety was fast possessing the public mind when another alarm was given.

Rumours came that fully five thousand Sioux warriors were encamped only a few miles distant; that they were preparing for an attack on the settlement in overwhelming numbers. A panic seized the settlers. It was decided that the best and safest way was for all to leave the country, taking along such articles as they could carry in their wagons, and remain away until the savages had dispersed.

When the time came for our family to go I remembered an old hen, with a brood of young chickens, which I wished very much to take with me, as I feared they would be killed by the Indians or die of starvation. But no room for them could be found in the wagon, so I ran out just before we started to take a farewell look, and lingered to pound for them some extra ears of corn, as they were too small to eat whole kernels, and there being no mills within seventy miles the corn had to be cracked for them. With tearful eyes I parted from my chickens and took my place in the wagon, terrified with thoughts of the vicious Sioux, who were the cause of so much trouble. During the journey the company was constantly annoyed by reports that the Indians were coming in by thousands, throwing up intrenchments, and giving abundant evidence that they meant to exterminate the settlers and gain possession of the country. These reports the more readily gained currency because of the fact that the Indians while in the vicinity constructed rifle pits, that were distinctly visible many years afterward.

When a location was reached, too distant for immediate danger, a halt was made. This was near what is now called Nora Springs, on the Shell Rock River. Here a suitable site for a camp was selected, where the entire company remained three weeks, in intense fear and excitement, kept up by continual reports of the presence and threatening attitude of the Sioux. A vigilant watch was kept day and night, as no one knew what hour the dreaded foe might come upon us.

But as no Indians had been seen on the journey, nor after we reached this place, confidence in the reports began to wane, and it was thought best to send out scouts to ascertain the truth. Accordingly Mr. Dickerson and father started for the lake, keeping ever on the alert for the wily foe, lest they should be killed or captured. Their return was awaited with no little concern and anxiety. When they arrived, however, they brought the cheering news that they had not encountered a single Indian, and had been most happily surprised to find their homes just as they had left them. Indeed there was nothing to indicate that the savages had been there.

The camp on the Shell Rock was immediately deserted, and the settlers returned to the homes they had so hastily abandoned. We reached our own place about dark. The first thing I did was to run to the barn to see my pets. The old hen was gone, but the chickens which in three weeks had grown nearly out of my knowledge were all nestled together in their accustomed corner.

CHAPTER 4

On to Okoboji

The next season my father sold his house and land. Not yet having found the object of his wishes, another move was made to Dickinson County, in the North-western part of the state. The sum derived from the sale of the property at Clear Lake enabled father to purchase several yoke of oxen, a number of cows, and quite a herd of young cattle; still reserving enough means to provide for the family until new land Could be located and crops raised.

Bidding *adieu* to the dear friends at Clear Lake, with whom we had shared so many privations, hardships, and dangers during the sixteen months we had tarried there, we again took up our line of march, in company with Harvey Luce and family, now consisting of himself, wife, and two children—Albert, aged four years, and Amanda, one year. Our journey extended this time into the beautiful region of Spirit and Okoboji Lakes. About this time, this place began to be viewed as the "promised land" of the adventurous pioneer; although there were yet no settlers in the county.

On the route taken, no traces of civilization were discernible west of Algona in Kossuth County. The Des Moines River was unbridged, and the sloughs being filled with water were frequently impassable. On the way we frequently encountered the "red skins" by day, and were entertained at night by the howling of wolves. Still we went forward unhesitatingly in our lonely journey; driving the slow-footed oxen and wagons, loaded with household goods, agricultural implements, and provisions, making our own road over many miles of desolate prairie. The traveller of today, with the easy and rapid mode of transit through the cultivated fields of Iowa, can scarcely have a just conception of the tediousness and hardships experienced by the early immigrants, as they plodded along day by day and slept at night by a campfire.

Still the journey through this wild, romantic country—to one whose eyes were open to receive it—brought much that was enjoyable. There were many things to break the monotony of the journey; things not only calculated to awaken the mind of a child; but worthy the attention of the scientist and the sage. The far stretching prairie, clothed in its mantle of green, luxuriant grass, studded here and there with the golden stars of the resin-weed; and a thousand flowering plants of a humbler growth but no less brilliant hues, presented to the eye a scene of enchanting beauty, beside which the things of man's devising fade like stars before the morning sun. Nor were prairies the only attraction. Here and there a babbling brook and sparkling river came together, eager to join hands and be away to the sea; and along their banks were shady groves of maple, oak, and elm, festooned with wild grape, woodbine, bitter-sweet, and ivy, in most fantastic forms and prodigality. Herds of elk and deer, in all the grace of their native freedom, fed on the nutritious grasses, and sought shelter in groves. Every variety of wild fowl—in flocks which no man could number—filled the air and nested on the ground. In fact every spot teemed with life and beauty. All this filled our hearts with that peaceful joy which nature gives.

July 16, 1856, the heavy emigrant wagons, after a journey of one hundred and ten miles, brought their passengers to the shores of the Okoboji Lakes. Seldom, before this, had the numerous beauties of these lovely lakes greeted the eye of a white man. Their waters had slept for centuries unknown to the turmoils of civilization, disturbed only by their finny inhabitants, flocks of wild fowl, or the rippling oars of the Indian's canoe. Schools of perch, bass, pike, pickerel, and many other fish, common to this region, had long gambolled below their transparent surface without fear of the white man; while the swan, proudly curving her graceful neck, floated her snowy bosom above them exulting in a realm where she reigned sole monarch.

Dickinson County was named in honour of Daniel S. Dickinson, at that time a senator of the United States from the State of New York. It contains a beautiful chain of lakes covering about ten thousand acres, besides smaller sheets of water, twenty-five in number, scattered over its surface, most of them being perfect gems of beauty. The largest of these is Spirit Lake, the Indian name being "*Minne-Waukon*," signifying, spirit water. Its shape is oblong; its greatest length or width is four miles. One is enabled to see the whole lake at one glance, from any point along the line of bluffs that border the western shore. Its sloping gravelly beach, its picturesque hills and shady groves extending west, and its wide rolling prairies on the east, give a variety and beauty of scenery, of which the eye is never weary. Tradition says the Indians regarded this lake with a superstitious awe; they believed its waters were haunted by spirits, and that no Dakota ever ventured to cross it in his canoe.

The Okoboji Lakes retain the Indian name, which signifies "a place of rest." East Okoboji commences at the foot of Spirit Lake, from which it is separated by a narrow isthmus, and runs south-easterly a distance of about six miles. It has the general appearance of a wide, gently flowing, and peaceful river, more than that of a lake. Its level is about four feet lower than that of Spirit Lake. These two lakes, East and West Okoboji, when taken in connection with Spirit Lake, afford opportunity for seventy-five miles of navigation. West Okoboji is the most beautiful lake in the Northwest. It is said by many to be the most beautiful of all the lakes in the United States; others have said that it possesses similar attributes of loveliness to those found in Zurich and Lucerne of Switzerland. Its waters have been sounded to a depth of two hundred and fifty feet. They are so clear and transparent that objects are distinguishable to a depth of fifty feet. It has numerous capes, bays, and promontories. Along its shores are precipitous banks and abrupt headlands; while its sloping, gravelly beaches cannot be surpassed for loveliness. Along these graceful curves, sailboats and steamers now bear thousands of enchanted tourists every season.

Such were the charming scenery and delightful surroundings amidst which my father established his last earthly home. Truly its loveliness was enough to reward him for all his previous toils and changes; and he felt that here, at last, he might settle, and spend the evening of his days in quiet. The feelings of his heart, at this time, are beautifully expressed by the poet:

In all my wanderings, around this world of care,
In all my griefs—and God has given me my share—
I still had hopes my latest hours to crown;
Amidst these humble bowers to lay me down;
To husband out life's taper at the close,
And keep the flame from wasting by repose.
I still had hopes—for pride attends us still—
Around my fire, an evening group to draw,

And tell of all I felt, and all I saw;
And as a hare, whom hounds and horns pursue,
Pants to the place from whence she flew,
I still had hopes, my long vexations past,
Here to remain, and die at home at last.

CHAPTER 5

Dickinson County Settlement and Adjacent Settlements

Soon after we arrived at the lakes, we heard the report of fire-arms in the groves around us; but whether it came from the rifle of the white man, or the red man, we knew not; but to our delight a company of whites was found encamped near the strait on the north side of West Okoboji. The party consisted of four men, namely, Wm. Granger, Carl Granger, Bertell A. Snyder, and Dr. I. H. Harriott. They were all, except Wm. Granger, young men without families, and his family was not with him.

They came from Red Wing, Minn., to seek for themselves homes in this "forest primeval." They were now engaged in the pleasing sports of hunting and fishing; enjoying the wild, romantic charms which nature had here lavished in such profusion. They were the first white men to paddle a canoe over the deep blue waters of the Okobojis.

After my father and Mr. Luce had spent two or three days pros-pecting, they decided to locate on the south side of West Okoboji. Accordingly on this site our tents, which sheltered the families till one log house was erected, were pitched. This house stood (and still stands) a few rods from the lake, on a rise of ground, covered by a dense grove of oaks. It fronted southward, and looked out upon a wide stretch of rolling prairie.

As July was too late for planting crops, little could be done before the approach of winter, except breaking some prairie for crops the next spring, making hay, and providing shelter for the cattle. Not able yet to supply themselves with anything from their new land, they were dependent upon Fort Dodge, eighty miles southeast, for all their provisions.

As soon as time would permit, Mr. Luce began another log cabin, for himself and family, nearby, on an adjoining piece of land, east of father's; but being unable to finish his house before the approach of winter, the first dwelling ever erected in Dickinson County—my father's—was the abode of both families during the winter. Father, mother, sister Eliza, (aged sixteen,) myself, (aged thirteen,) brother Rowland, (aged six,) and Mr. and Mrs. Luce, with their two children, comprised the inmates of that sturdy cottage.

Not long were we thus alone, in this new found "Eldorado." Knowledge of its rich lands, luxuriant groves, abundant game and fish, its beautiful scenery and healthful climate, soon reached many who had a love for adventure; so that by the first of November six families were snugly housed in log cabins, within six miles of us; besides several single men in the settlement.

Dr. Harriott, Bert Snyder, and the two Granger brothers erected a cabin on the peninsula between the two Okobojis, north of the strait, now known as "Smith's Point." The Chicago, Milwaukee & St. Paul R. R. now passes directly over the ground where their cabin stood. James Mattock, with wife and five children, came from Delaware county, and established a home, south of the strait, nearly opposite the Granger cabin. These two dwellings stood in close proximity to each other. There was also residing with Mr. Mattock a man by the name of Madison. Mr. Madison had brought with him one son, about eighteen years old. His wife, and several other of their children, remained in Delaware county, expecting to come in the spring.

Joel Howe's family consisted of himself, wife, and six children; besides four married children who were not at this time members of his household, and only one, Mrs. Nobles, was in the settlement. He settled on the east side of East Okoboji, at the south side of the grove, near the present residence of Peter Ladue. The names and ages of their children were as follows: Jonathan, aged twenty-three, Sardis, eighteen, Alfred, fifteen, Jacob, thirteen, Philetus, eleven, and Levi, nine. Alvin Noble, son-in-law of Joel Howe, with his wife and one child, some two years old, and Joseph M. Thatcher, with wife and one child, seven months old, came with the family of Mr. Howe, from Hampton, Franklyn County. They were formerly from Howard County, Indiana. These two families also settled on the east side of East Okoboji, erecting one log cabin, which was occupied by both families. Their cabin was at the north end of the grove, about one mile from the home of Mr. Howe. This cabin is still standing upon the farm of Mr. H. D.

Arthur, a few rods north of his house, (as at time of first publication).

There was also, residing for the winter with Messrs Noble and Thatcher, a man by the name of Morris Markham, who also came from Hampton, and originally from Howard county, Indiana.

Mr. Marble and wife, who came from Linn County, were the first and at this time the only settlers on Spirit Lake. Their location was on the west shore of the lake, about four miles from the present town of Spirit Lake, in the south edge of what has since been known as Marble Grove.

Thus forty persons—men, women, and children—were dispersed among the picturesque groves, bluffs, and lakes of Dickinson County, where the chief scenes of this narrative transpired. As we dwell on the events connected with the first settlement of this county, we are impressed with the heroic courage of those early pioneers, who turned their backs upon civilization and its comforts, and placed so many miles between themselves and the settled portion of the state for the sake of a home in the romantic region of these beautiful lakes; for, let it be remembered, there were at this time, no settlements west of these; and the nearest on the northeast were on the Minnesota and Watonwan Rivers. A few families that year (1856) settled on the west branch of the Des Moines, in Palo Alto and Emmet counties.

On the Little Sioux, which has its source in Minnesota, flowing south westwardly to the Missouri River, passing some five or six miles west of Spirit Lake, was the settlement of Smithland in Woodbury County. At what is now called Correctionville, about twenty miles farther up the stream, a few families had also settled. In Clay County, about forty miles south of the lakes, some six or eight families had located—being the last in that direction in the state. In the same year (1856) six or seven families located eighteen miles north of the lakes, on the head waters of the Des Moines, in Jackson County, Minnesota, where a town was laid out and called Springfield (now Jackson).

These were the nearest neighbours to the Dickinson County settlers. Among the principal parties in the Springfield settlement were three brothers—William, Charles, and George Wood, of Mankato, Minnesota, who laid out the town and opened a store. All these settlements were on the extreme frontier, and absolutely unprotected and defenceless; but the fact that in the spring of 1855 the Indians had generally withdrawn from the Upper Des Moines and the lakes in Dickinson County, had encouraged the hope that all danger from them had passed.

On one occasion, while on a trip to Fort Dodge, father fell in with a Dr. Strong, and prevailed upon him to visit the lakes with a view to settlement; but after stopping with us a few days he decided to locate at Springfield. His family consisted of himself, wife, and one child (two years old). His wife being in delicate health, and he necessarily being away much of the time from home, she persuaded my sister Eliza, to whom she became attached, to accompany them. This was in the month of October, and owing to a heavy fall of snow, on the first of December, followed by others in quick succession, until the snow on the level was four or five feet deep, and in the drifts sometimes fifteen or twenty, travelling was impossible. Eliza was thus unable to return, and so escaped the fate of the rest of the family.

The winter of 1856-7 was one ever to be remembered by the people of Iowa and Minnesota for its bitter cold weather, deep snow, and violent storms, rendering communication between the different settlements almost impossible. Of course the settlers were illy prepared for any winter, and much less for such a one as this; for it must be remembered there was no lumber to be had within a hundred miles, and all the provisions, of every kind, except what might be captured from the lakes and groves, had to be brought a like distance. Some cabins were yet without floors; the doors were made of puncheons, hung on wooden hinges, and fastened with wooden latches. Our floor was made comfortable by levelling off the ground and covering it with prairie hay, over which a rag carpet was spread, which had been brought all the way from the state of New York.

With inexpressible sadness I now recall some of the scenes and events that transpired in that humble but happy home; when, from some good book, Mrs. Luce read aloud to the family, or, perhaps, father was solving a problem for me in arithmetic, while my little brother was seated at the table, trying to form letters from a copy written by sister Eliza; and mother in her rocking-chair was crocheting, or, perhaps, fashioning a garment into shape for some member of the household. Little did I dream that all the bright prospects of my youth would so soon be nipped in the bud—blasted as by an untimely frost, and our quiet home become the scene of one of the most cruel, barbarous massacres ever recorded on the bloody pages of history.

In February, Mr. Luce and Mr. Thatcher started, with an ox-team and sled, to obtain provisions for their families. In spite of snow-banks, sometimes fifteen and twenty feet deep; in spite of wind and cold; they reached Hampton, Shell Rock, Cedar Falls, and Waterloo. They secured as large a supply as they thought possible to convey, with their weary oxen, over the untrodden drifts; and succeeded in making their way back as far as Shippey's cabin, in Palo Alto county, about ten miles below Ernmetsburg, on the Des Moines River. Here it was decided that Mr. Thatcher should remain to recruit the oxen, while Mr. Luce proceeded home, accompanied by three young men, who were making their first visit to the lakes—Jonathan Howe and Enoch Ryan, (son and son-in-law of Joel Howe,) of Hampton, and one of the name of Clark, from Waterloo. Little did they imagine that they were going to meet such a cruel death. By this delay of Mr. Thatcher he escaped the terrible fate of the doomed colony at the lakes.

It was now drawing toward the close of a long, cold, and dreary winter. These brave pioneers were looking hopefully forward to the time when they should go forth to the pleasant task of cultivating their farms and improving their homes; for as yet no Indians had appeared, and no reports of their coming had reached them to awaken suspicion or disturb their repose.

W. OKOBOJI LAKE.

CHAPTER 6

Ink-Pa-Du-Ta and His Band

In order to understand the events recorded in these pages, it is necessary to have some knowledge of Inkpaduta, the chief, under whose leadership was perpetrated the bloody massacre of March, 1857. In giving this, I have drawn freely from the authentic documents prepared by Charles E. Flandreau, then U. S. Indian agent for the Sioux, and Major Prichette, special government agent. In an exhaustive paper read by Judge Flandreau before the Minnesota State Historical Society, in December, 1879, he gave the following account of Inkpaduta:

Prior to 1842, the Sac and Fox tribes of Indians occupied the country which is now the State of Iowa. On the 11th of October, 1842, these Indians made a treaty with the United States government, by which they sold the land west of the Mississippi river to which they had claim or title, or in which they had any interest whatever; reserving the right of occupancy, for three years from the date of the treaty, to all that part of the lands ceded which lay west of a line running due north and south from the Painted or Red Rocks, on the White Breast Fork of the Des Moines River, which rocks were situated eight miles from the junction of the White Breast with the Des Moines. The country north of Iowa, and west of the Mississippi River, as far as the Little Rapids on the Minnesota River, was occupied by the Medewakanton and Wakpekuti bands of Sioux Indians. These latter Indians were at war with the Sacs and Foxes. The Wakpekuti band was under the leadership of two principal chiefs, named Wamdisapa and Tasagi. The lawless and predatory habits of Wamdisapa and his band prolonged the war with the Sacs and Foxes; and to a great extent created difficulties between the band of Wamdisapa and the rest of the Wakpekuti, which troubles gradually separated his band from them. Wamdisapa and his people moved to the west, toward the Missouri, and occupied the land about the Vermillion River. So thoroughly was he separated from the rest of the Wakpekutis that when the last named Indians together with the Medewakantons made their treaty at Mendota, in 1851, by which they ceded the lands in Minnesota owned by them, the remnant of Wamdisapa's people were not regarded as being part of the Wakpekutis at all, and took no part in the treaty.

By 1857, all that remained of Wamdisapa's band was under the chieftainship of Inkpaduta, or Scarlet Point, sometimes called Red End. In August, 1856, I received the appointment of United States Indian agent for the Sioux of the Mississippi. The agencies of these Indians were on the Minnesota River at Redwood, and on the Yellow Medicine River, a few miles from its mouth. Having been on the frontier for some time previous to such appointment, I had become quite familiar with the Sioux, and knew, in a general way, of Inkpaduta and his band, its habits and whereabouts. They ranged the country far and wide, and were considered a bad lot of vagabonds. In 1856 they came to the payment and demanded a share of the money of the Wakpekuti band, and made a great deal of trouble, but were forced to return to their haunts, on the Big Sioux and adjoining country.

According to the most authentic testimony collected by Major Prichette, Inkpaduta came to the Sioux Agency in the fall of 1855 and received annuities for eleven persons, although he was not identified with any band.

He had killed the chief of the Wakpekuti band, Tasagi, with several of his relatives, and was declared an outlaw by the band; but was permitted to receive payment with them, from fear, they said, of revenge in case it was denied.

He supported himself by hunting and plunder; leading a wandering, marauding life, the number of his followers varying from time to time from fifty to one hundred and fifty; as individuals of similar character, from different bands of Sioux, joined or deserted him.

I give below, as far as I know, the names of this band at the time of the Spirit Lake massacre:

Ink-pa-du-ta., or Scarlet Point.

Mak-pe-a-ho-to-man, or Roaring Cloud, and Mak-pi-op-e-ta, or
Fire Cloud, twins.

Taw-a-che-ha-wa-kan, or His Mysterious Father.

Ba-ha-ta, or Old Man.

Ke-cho-mon, or Putting on as he walks.

Ka-ha-dat, or Ratling (son-in-law of Inkpaduta).

Fe-to-a-ton-ka, or Big Face.

Ta-te-li-da-shink-sha-man-i, or One who makes a crooked
wind as he walks.

Ta-chan-che-ga-ho-ta, or His Great Gun.

Hu-san, or One Leg.

As I remember Inkpaduta, he was probably fifty or sixty years of
age, about six feet in height, and strongly built. He was deeply pitted
by small pox, giving him a revolting appearance, and distinguishing
him from the rest of the band. His family consisted of himself and
squaw, four sons, and one daughter. His natural enmity to the white
man; his desperately bold and revengeful disposition; his hatred of his
enemies, even of his own race; his matchless success on the war-path,
won for him honour from his people, distinguished him as a hero, and
made him a leader of his race.

By the whites—especially those who have escaped the scenes of
his brutal carnage, to wear, within, the garb of deepest mourning, from
the severing of social, parental, and filial ties—Inkpaduta will ever be
remembered as a savage monster in human shape, fitted only for the
darkest corner in Hades.

From the landing of the Pilgrim Fathers on the rock-bound coast
of New England, in 1620, until the present day, the native red men
have at different times given sad and fearful evidences of their protes-
tation against civilization's irresistible march across the American con-
tinent, but no other tribe of aborigines has ever exhibited more savage
ferocity or so appalled and sickened the soul of humanity by whole-
sale slaughtering of the white race as has the Sioux. The Sioux are
said to have had their name bestowed upon them by the French, but
they ignore the title and answer only to the name of Dakotas. They
number about 25,000 and are known as: Tetons, Sissetons, Yanktons,
Yanktonais, Wapetons, Wakpekutis, etc. These tribes are subdivided
into bands; each band having its own chief.

These Indians are widely diffused over a vast region of country west of the Missouri, clear up to the base of the Rocky Mountains, and possess immense tracts of good agricultural land in Dakota, sufficient in extent to allow eighty acres to each member, of the band, who is willing to adopt the pursuit of agriculture, which has long been neglected by this race. The Sioux are now all fed and cared for at an enormous expense by the government, (as at time of first publication).

CHAPTER 7

Circumstances that Led to the Massacre

In the autumn of 1856, Inkpaduta's band went down to the lower valley of the Little Sioux, where the first trouble with the whites began, in the vicinity of Smithland. Several aggressions by the Indians and violent repulses by the whites are given, as preceding the incidents, generally accepted by both Indians and whites, as the immediate cause of the fatal catastrophe.

It seems, that one day, while the Indians were in pursuit of elk, they had some difficulty with the settlers. The Indians claimed that the whites intercepted the chase. There is also a report that an Indian was bitten by a dog belonging to one of the settlers; that the Indian killed the dog; and that the man gave the Indian a severe beating. It is also said that the settlers whipped off a company of squaws, who were carrying off their hay and corn. The Indians becoming more and more insolent, the settlers, in self-protection, went to the camp and disarmed them, intending to return their guns the next day and escort them out of the country; but the next morning not a "red skin" was to be seen, they had folded their tents, "like the Arabs," and as silently stolen away. They went up the Little Sioux; their hearts filled with revenge, and committed depredations as they went. At first they pretended to be friendly, but soon commenced depredations, forcibly taking guns, ammunition, provisions, and whatever they wanted. They also amused themselves by discharging their guns through articles of furniture; ripping open feather beds and scattering their contents through the yards. The farther they proceeded, the fewer and more defenceless the settlers were; and the bolder and more insolent the Indians became.

After remaining a few days in Cherokee County, where they busied themselves with wantonly shooting cattle, hogs, and fowls, and destroying property generally; sometimes severely beating those who resisted, they proceeded up the Little Sioux, to the little settlement in Clay County, now called Peterson. Here they tarried two or three days, committing acts of atrocity as usual. At the house of A. S. Mead (Mr. Mead being away) they not only killed his cattle and destroyed his property, but knocked down his wife and carried off to their camp his daughter Hattie (seventeen years old); and started away with a younger sister, Emma, (ten years old), but she resisted so hard and cried so loud that an Indian picked up a stick and whipped her all the way back to the house and left her. At the same house they knocked down Mr. E. Taylor, kicked his boy into the fireplace—burning him so badly that he still carries the scar on his leg—and took his wife off to their camp; but as yet they had committed no murder.

After one night's experience in an Indian camp, Mrs. Taylor and Hattie Mead were permitted to return home. These blood-thirsty Indians, thus exasperated, and, naturally burning with hatred and revenge, still continued their tortuous journey, and by the evening of the seventh of March reached the vicinity of Okoboji Lakes. The settlers here had no knowledge of what had transpired down the valley. Nor through the long hours of that night when wrapped in peaceful repose, did the winds that soughed through the tops of the naked trees, and whistled around the corners of their cabins tell them; neither did they dream of the foul conspiracy that was brewing.

ABBIE GARDNER TAKEN CAPTIVE

CHAPTER 8

The Massacre

Oh, bloodiest picture in the book of Time;
Sarmatia fell, unwept, without a crime.

It will be remembered that Mr. Luce reached home, from his trip to Waterloo, on the evening of March 6th. Now that he was with his family, my father at once began preparations for a needed trip to Fort Dodge, also for provisions. These preparations were completed by the evening of the 7th, and on the morning of the 8th we arose earlier than usual, in order that father might have an early start, so as to make as much progress as practicable the first day, and gain, if possible, the cabin of some friendly settler for the night. But, alas! how little we know what lies before us. We know not what an hour, much less a day, may bring forth.

The sun never shed brighter beams of light than on that ill-fated morning. Spring, that had already come, in theory, seemed now to have come in reality. The winter of our discontent seemed indeed to have passed away. As we were about to surround the table for breakfast, a solitary Indian entered the house, wearing the guise of friendship and claiming the sacred prerogative of hospitality. A place was promptly prepared for him at the table, and he partook of the frugal meal with the family. This one was soon followed by others, until Inkpaduta and his fourteen warriors, with their squaws and *papooses*, had entered the house. They dissembled friendship, and the scanty store of the household was freely divided among them, until each seemed satisfied. They, then, became suddenly sullen, insolent, and overbearing, demanding ammunition and numerous other things. When father was giving one of them a few gun-caps, he snatched the whole box from his hand. At the same time another—as if by agreement—tried

38

to get a powder-horn hanging against the wall; but was prevented by Mr. Luce, who now suspected that their intention was to get the ammunition, that we might not be able to defend ourselves.

The Indian then drew up his gun, and would have shot Mr. Luce, had the latter not promptly seized the gun pointed at his head. About this time (9 o'clock, a. m.,) Dr. Harriott and Mr. Snyder called, knowing of father's intended trip to Fort Dodge, and wishing to send letters to be mailed. Father told them, at once, that he could not go and leave his family, as he feared the Indians were on the warpath, and thought the situation serious. He also told them that the other settlers ought to be notified of the danger, and immediate arrangements made for defence. Our house, being the largest and strongest in the colony, his plan was to have the other settlers gather there. But Dr. Harriott and Mr. Snyder thought it was only a pet of the Indians and would soon pass away; so they did some trading with them, and returned to their own cabin, taking no precautions, whatever, for safety. The Indians prowled around with every manifestation of arrogance and insolence, until noon, when they went off toward Mr. Mattock's. They drove our cattle before them, and shot them on the way.

This was the first time the house had been clear of Indians since they first entered, in the morning. A consultation was then held, as to what should be done. It was the desire to notify the other settlers; but if any went to do this it would weaken the force at home; and the Indians were liable to return at any moment; besides, from the direction taken by the Indians, it was almost impossible to reach the other cabins without being discovered by the (now known to be) malignant foe. However, philanthropic considerations prevailed; and it was finally decided that Mr. Luce and Mr. Clark should go to warn the others of the impending danger, while father should remain at home, to defend, as well as possible, the family, in any emergency.

According to this arrangement they started out about 2 p. m., never to return. My sister, remembering the attempt of the Indians to take the life of her husband in the morning, twined her arms around his neck, and weeping said: "O, Harvey! I am afraid you will never come back to me! the Indians will kill you if they don't anyone else." This was, indeed, their last parting. About three o'clock we heard the report of guns, in rapid succession, from the house of Mr. Mattock. We were, then, no longer in doubt as to the awful reality that was hanging over us. Two long hours we passed in this fearful anxiety and suspense, waiting and watching, with conflicting hopes and fears, for Mr. Luce and Mr. Clark to return.

At length, just as the sun was sinking behind the western horizon, shedding its brilliant rays over the snowy landscape, father, whose anxiety would no longer allow him to remain within doors, went out to reconnoitre. He, however, hastily returned, saying: "Nine Indians are coming, now only a short distance from the house, and we are all doomed to die." His first thought was to barricade the door and fight till the last, saying: "While they are killing all of us, I will kill a few of them, with the two loaded guns still left in the house."

But to this mother protested, having not yet lost all faith in the savage monsters, and still hoping they would appreciate our kindness and spare our lives, she said: "If we have to die, let us die innocent of shedding blood."

Alas, for the faith placed in these inhuman monsters! They entered the house and demanded more flour; and, as father turned to get them what remained of our scanty store, they shot him through the heart; he fell upon his right side and died without a struggle. When first the Indian raised his gun to fire, mother or Mrs. Luce seized the gun and drew it down; but the other Indians instantly turned upon them, seized them by their arms, and beat them over the head with the butts of their guns; then dragged them out of doors, and killed them in the most cruel and shocking manner.

They then began an indiscriminate destruction of everything in the house; breaking open trunks and taking out clothing, cutting open feather-beds, and scattering the feathers everywhere. When the Indians entered the house, and during these awful scenes, I was seated in a chair, holding my sister's baby in my arms; her little boy on one side, and my little brother on the other, clinging to me in terror. They next seized the children; tearing them from me one by one, while they reached their little arms to me, crying piteously for protection that I was powerless to give. Heedless of their cries, they dragged them out of doors, and beat them to death with sticks of stove-wood.

All this time I was both speechless and tearless; but, now left alone, I begged them to kill me. It seemed as though I could not wait for them to finish their work of death. One of them approached, and roughly seizing me by the arm said something I could not understand, but I well knew, from their actions, that I was to be a captive. All the terrible tortures and indignities I had ever read or heard of being inflicted upon their captives now arose in horrid vividness before me.

After ransacking the house, and taking whatever they thought might be serviceable, such as provisions, bedding, arms, and ammunition; and after the bloody scalping knife had done its terrible work; I was dragged from the never-to-be-forgotten scene. No language can ever suggest, much less adequately portray, my feelings as I passed that door.

With a naturally sensitive nature, tenderly and affectionately reared, shuddering at the very thought of cruelty, you can, my dear reader, imagine, but only imagine, the agony I endured, when so suddenly plunged into scenes from which no element of the terrible or revolting seemed wanting. Behind me I left my heroic father, murdered in a cowardly manner, in the very act of extreme hospitality; shot down at my feet, and I had not the privilege of impressing one farewell kiss upon his lips, yet warm with life and affection. Just outside the door lay the three children—so dear to me—bruised, mangled, and bleeding; while their moans and groans pierced my ears, and called in vain for one loving caress which I was prevented from giving them.

A little farther on lay my Christ-like mother, who till the very last had pleaded the cause of her brutish murderers, literally weltering in her own blood. Still farther on, at the southwest corner of the house, in a similar condition, lay my eldest sister, Mrs. Luce, who had been so intimately associated with me from earliest recollections. Amid these scenes of unutterable horror, I took my farewell look upon father, mother, sister, and brother, and my sister's little ones.

Filled with loathing for these wretches whose hands were still wet with the blood of those dearest to me, and at one of whose belts still hung the dripping scalp of my mother; with even the much coveted boon of death denied me, we plunged into the gloom of the forest and the coming night; but neither the gloom of the forest, nor the blackness of the night, nor both combined, could begin to symbolize the darkness of my terror-stricken heart.

Chapter 9

The Massacre Continued

Man's inhumanity to man
Makes countless millions mourn.

Terrible as were the scenes through which I had just passed, others, if possible even yet more horrible, awaited me. A tramp of about one mile brought me to the camp of my captors, which was the home of Mr. Mattock. Here the sights and sounds that met the eye and ear were truly appalling. The forest was lighted by the campfires, and also by the burning of the cabins; and the air was rent with the unearthly war-whoop of the savages, and the shrieks and groans of two helpless victims, confined in the burning cabin, suffering all the agonies of a fiery death. Scattered upon the ground was a number of bodies, among which I recognized that of Dr. Harriott, rifle still in hand; as well as the bodies of Mr. Mattock, Mr. Snyder, and others, with rifles near them, some broken. All gave evidence that an attempt at resistance had been made, but too late.

Dr. Harriott and Mr. Snyder, it seemed, had come across the strait from their home, to assist their neighbours. In all this affray not one Indian was killed, and only one wounded; but this one quite badly, and by Dr. Harriott, as the Indians told me. Here had perished five men, two women, and four children; and the bodies, save the two in the burning cabin, lay about the camp, their ghastly features clearly revealed by the light of the burning building; presenting a frightful scene beyond the power of my feeble pen to describe. Carl Granger's remains lay beside the Granger cabin. He had been first shot, and then his head chopped off above his mouth and ears, supposed to have been done with a broad-axe, found on the premises. Wm. Granger escaped the fate of his brother, being at home, at Red Wing, with his family.

Burning of Mr. Mattock's Cabin

Messrs. Clark and Luce were killed near the outlet on the southern shore of East Okoboji, a mile or more from father's cabin. It is probable that they had despaired of reaching the Mattock and Granger cabins, and had attempted to go around the southern end of East Okoboji, and so reach the cabins of Howe and Thatcher; but were overtaken and shot on the way. The body of Mr. Clark was identified by a memorandum book, found in his pocket by those who discovered the remains, sometime in June. Thus the day's slaughter summed up a total of twenty human lives.

The ravenous appetites of the savages had been satisfied by my father's generosity, and my mother's and sister's incessant cooking and serving. Their thirst for blood must have been well-nigh quenched. All this must be celebrated by the war-dance—that hideous revelry that seems to have been borrowed from the lowest depth of Tartarus. Near the ghastly corpses, and over the blood-stained snow; with blackened faces, and fierce and uncouth gestures; and with wild screams and yells, they circled round and round, keeping time to the dullest, dreariest, sound of drum and rattle, until complete exhaustion compelled them to desist.

None but those who have had a personal experience with Indian warfare can form a just conception of the terror which their war-dance is calculated to inspire. Amid such fearful scenes, I spent that long, long, sleepless night—the first of my captivity, and the thoughts that fired my brain, and oppressed my heart, can never be imagined, except by those who have suffered like pangs, and had them burned into their souls by a like experience.

One day's carnage only sharpened the savages' thirst for blood. Accordingly, at an early hour the next morning, the braves(?), having smeared their faces with black, (which, with the Sioux, means war,) started again on their work of slaughter. The four remaining families were busy with their domestic cares, not dreaming of aught amiss, while these terrible scenes were being enacted at their very doors.

The Indians had gone but a short distance on East Okoboji, when they met Mr. Howe, who was on his way to father's to borrow some flour. Him they shot, and severed his head from his body, the skull being found, some two years later, on the southern shore of the lake by a man named Ring. Thence they proceeded to the house of Mr. Howe, where they found his wife, his son Jonathan, his daughter Sardis, a young lady, and four younger children. They left only lifeless bodies, here, to tell the story of their bloody work. From here they went to the cabin of Noble and Thatcher, where were two men and two women—Mr. and Mrs. Noble, Mr. Ryan, and Mrs. Thatcher, besides two children. With their usual cowardice and hypocrisy, the Indians feigned friendship until they had secured every advantage, so their own heads would be in no danger. Then, by concert of action, the two men were simultaneously shot. Ryan fell dead instantly. Mr. Noble cried, "O, I am killed!" After the fatal bullet struck him, he walked to the door, though bleeding freely, and then fell dead. They next seized the children by the feet, dragging them from their mothers' arms out of doors, and dashed their brains out against an oak tree which stood near the house. They then plundered the house, appropriating to themselves whatever they wanted.

After slaughtering the cattle, hogs, and poultry, they took the two women—Mrs. Noble and Mrs. Thatcher—captives, and started back to their camp. On their way they again stopped at the house of Mr. Howe. Here a terrible spectacle met the gaze of the captives. Mrs. Noble found her mother lying dead under the bed, where she had doubtless crawled after being left by her brutal murderers. Her head was terribly beaten, probably with a flatiron, as one lay nearby bearing traces of the murderous work. The eyes were protruding from the sockets, and as Mrs. Noble described them "looked like balls of fire." Her brother Jacob, some thirteen years old, who had been left for dead or dying, was found sitting up out in the yard, and conscious, although unable to speak. To her questions he responded only with a nod or a shake of the head. She told him, if the Indians did not come to him and finish the murder, to crawl into the house and get into one of the beds, as perhaps help would come and he might be saved; but the savages made sure of their work before they left, killing him before her eyes. The rest of the family lay scattered about the house and yard, all more or less mutilated. While Mrs. Noble was taking note of these things, the Indians were busy with their work of plunder and destruction; after which, with captives and booty, they returned to their camp.

Immediately upon their arrival, I was taken to the tent where were my two companions in captivity; and we were permitted, for the space of half or three-quarters of an hour, to recount our losses, and the terrible scenes through which we had just passed. Then each one was taken to a separate lodge, and by signs and gestures told to braid our hair, and paint our faces, after the fashion of squaws.

The terrible calamity that had fallen upon me seemed more than

I could bear, and as I now look back upon it I wonder that I survived; wonder that either body or mind, or both, did not give way. In the impressive language of Longfellow:

The burden laid upon me,
Seemed greater than I could bear.

Snatched from the society of loving friends and the tender care of affectionate parents; and plunged into hopeless, helpless servitude to these inhuman, fiendish monsters, whom I had seen brutally murder those so dear to me, and whom I consequently could only abhor, Oh! how I longed for death; and whenever they thought to torture me by threatening to take my life, I would merely bow my head. My tearless acquiescence and willingness to die seemed to fill them with wonder, and even admiration, as they thought it a sign of great bravery, a quality they highly appreciate but which they did not suppose the white woman to possess. Soon after my capture, one of the warriors, who was sitting by me one day in the tent, thinking to test my courage or to be amused at my fears, took his revolver from his belt and began loading it, while he gave me to understand that he would kill me as soon as it was loaded. I merely bowed my head to signify that I was ready.

When the revolver was all loaded he drew back the hammer and pointed it close to my head, but again I quietly bowed my head expecting he would do as he said; but instead of that he lowered the weapon, and looked at me as though astonished, and then laughed at me uproariously. So amused was he, indeed, that when others came into the *teepe* he would tell them the story, by signs and gesture, of how I had acted. Nor did it stop here, but for days after I could see that it was a favourite topic of conversation among them, and never again, except once by a squaw, was a weapon drawn upon me while I was a captive.

So utterly ignorant were these savages of all the arts of civilized life, that they were at a loss to know what to do with all the plunder that curiosity or cupidity had prompted them to take. Among the spoils were quantities of soda and cream of tartar. They interrogated me as to their use; and when I told them we used it in making bread they wished me to make some, using these articles. They seemed greatly surprised and pleased when they saw the bread "grow" during the process of baking. Doubtless had I been older and more wily, I could have made them believe I was a "big medicine," and had power to work miracles; so might have gotten from them any favours I might have desired; but I was so completely overwhelmed and subdued with grief that I had no thought or heart for such tricks.

So interested were they about the bread "growing," that when others came into the *teepe* those who had witnessed the wonderful phenomenon described it with the grotesque gesticulations peculiar to their race. Although pleased with the "growing," they were too suspicious of being poisoned to eat any themselves until I had eaten of it. Finding that I was willing to eat it, they greedily devoured it, without waiting to see what its effect on me might be.

On the morning of the 10th they broke camp, and crossed West Okoboji on the ice. Travelling to the westward a distance of three miles, they went into camp on the Madison claim. They had brought horses and sleds which they had taken from the settlers along the Little Sioux; also what they had found at the lakes. In this first movement after my capture, I was detailed to drive one of the teams; but it was the last time I had the privilege of riding until I was delivered into the hands of my rescuers.

The next day, at an early hour they tore down their tents and loaded their horses, squaws, dogs, and captives, and moved northwestwardly to Marble's Grove, on the west side of Spirit Lake. The Indians seemed to have been ignorant of the fact that there were any more whites in the neighbourhood until the 13th, when they no doubt accidentally discovered the cabin of Mr. Marble. He was not aware of their presence, and knew nothing of the massacre. Consequently he and his family were taken entirely by surprise when the Indians made their appearance.

Feigning friendship, they readily gained admission to the house; when, as usual, they asked for food. After satisfying their hunger, they bantered him to trade rifles. After the trade was made, they proposed to shoot at a mark. A board was set up, and after firing several shots it was knocked down. Mr. Marble's gun being empty, they requested him to set it up. As soon as his back was turned, they shot him through the back, and he fell dead in his tracks. Mrs. Marble was sitting at the window, with palpitating heart, watching their actions; and as soon as she saw her husband start to replace the board, as if by instinct, she divined their murderous intentions. Seeing him fall, she rushed for the door, and would have fled for her life; but was quickly overtaken and conveyed to the camp.

Thus, another unfortunate victim was added to our little band of helpless captives. We were all brought together in the same *tepee*; for what savage purpose we were at loss to know; unless it was that we might communicate to each other all their deeds of blood and plunder; for of these they were exceedingly proud, never losing an opportunity to recount them and glory in them. They carried away what they wanted from Mr. Marble's place, and destroyed what they could.

Mr. Marble was, probably, a stone-cutter by trade, as his implements were found in a hollow tree, near the house, by one of the early settlers. At night, this bloody day's work was celebrated by the "war-dance." Before leaving Marble's Grove, the Indians peeled the bark from a large tree, and on the white surface, with black paint, pictured, in hieroglyphical signs, the work they had done in Dickinson County. The number of persons killed were represented so as to indicate the position in which they were left. Men were represented as pierced by arrows, etc. Mattock's cabin was pictured with flames and smoke issuing from the roof; but whether by signs known to savage art they indicated that two helpless victims perished in the flames, I know not. This picture history was visible years afterward, and was familiar to the early settlers. Thus, it will be seen that Mr. Marble was the only person killed on Spirit Lake. Notwithstanding this tragic event has always been called, "the Spirit Lake massacre," from the fact that at this time the whole lake region was merely known abroad as Spirit Lake.

CHAPTER 10

Discovery of the Massacre

The massacre was first discovered by Mr. Markham. A yoke of oxen of his had strayed away in the fall, and he had failed to get any knowledge of their whereabouts until the return of Mr. Luce, which, the reader will remember, occurred on the 6th of March. On the morning of the 7th, Mr. Markham started for the Des Moines River in search of the cattle; and returned to my father's house about eleven o'clock on the evening of the 9th, cold, hungry, and exhausted, expecting a hospitable welcome to a happy home. He was surprised, indeed, to find the house dark and silent; and upon looking about he saw the dead bodies of my mother and sister, lying in the yard. Being satisfied that it was the work of the Indians, he carefully withdrew in the direction of Mr. Mattock's.

As the timber and underbrush were quite thick, he found himself almost in the midst of the Indian's camp before he was aware of it—so near, in fact, that he could hear their voices inside the *teepes*. He attracted the attention of the Indian's dogs, so that they began barking. He succeeded, however, in retracing his steps, without being noticed by the Indians, who at this late hour were all inside their lodges. Mr. Markham next wended his way to the house of Mr. Howe, where a like desolation awaited him. Sadly, wearily, he pushed on to the cabin of Noble and Thatcher, which was also his own home; but, oh, what a home! and what a reception! The cold, lifeless bodies of his friends was all that remained to welcome him.

Since morning, he had travelled some thirty miles over the trackless prairie, and through the drifted snow, without rest or refreshment; but so shocked was he by the scenes in the houses, that he preferred to spend the remainder of the night in the forest; so, gathering up a few pieces of broken furniture with which to kindle a fire, he withdrew to a deep ravine, a short distance from the house. Here, of course, it was impossible to lie down; so he was compelled to stand upon his already frozen and still freezing feet, and await the dawn.

The morning light only revealed, more distinctly, the terrible desolation which had been wrought during his absence. Supposing that Mr. Marble and family had shared the fate of the others, and consequently there were no whites nearer than Springfield, (now Jackson,) eighteen miles or more to the northward, famished and frozen as he was, he struggled on, and carried to my sister, and others there the terrible message.

The news fell with a crushing weight upon my sister, who now supposed she was the only one left of our family; not knowing yet that I was a captive. At first, only some general information of the massacre was told her; but finding that suspense and uncertainty were worse for her than the facts, especially as her suspicions were aroused by conversation she overheard, they told her plainly the terrible truth. To have heard of the sudden death of one member of the family, while she was absent, would have been sorrow indeed; but it was overwhelming to find that not one of her father's family was left, all having been swept away by one fell stroke of merciless savagery. Her situation was, indeed, one of indescribable affliction.

No kind father to welcome her home! No affectionate mother could ever again soothe her sorrow, or kiss away her tears! Never again could she gather, with her loving sisters and dear little brother, in that once so happy family circle dearest spot on earth to her! So suddenly and unexpectedly came the terrible news to her that it seemed wonderful that her reason was not dethroned. Her grief was greatly augmented by fearing that the Indians had taken me away; for she remembered that they wanted to trade some ponies for me, on one occasion, at Clear Lake. In her lamentations, she was frequently heard to say: "Oh! if I could only know where Abbie is, or what has been her fate, I could be more contented."

Upon hearing of the outbreak at the lakes, several families about Springfield assembled at the house of a Mr. Thomas for mutual defence, and immediately sent two men—Henry Tretts and Mr. Chiffen—with a petition to Fort Ridgeley, to ask that the United States troops be sent to their rescue. Among the settlers of Springfield there were two men named respectively Smith and Henderson, who, at this time, had their limbs frozen so badly that they had to be amputated, Henderson losing both legs and Smith one.

Several other persons awaited with them their fate, in the cabin of Mr. Wheeler. Wm. and George Wood—being influenced by the apparently friendly character of the Indians, with whom they had been trading for several months, as they had also with Inkpaduta's band, when on their way down the Little Sioux—could not believe the startling reports; or that there was really danger; so they remained in their store and lost their lives. George seemed to have had his doubts as to the safety of remaining at their posts; but was overpersuaded by his brother William. So positive was he that there was no danger, that against the remonstrance of the settlers, only a few days before the attack, he sold the Indians ammunition; receiving in payment money, which no doubt had been taken from the murdered citizens at the lakes.

In the fall of 1856, a small party of Sioux Indians came and pitched their tents in the neighbourhood of Springfield. There was also a large band, under the chieftainship of Ishtahabah, or Sleepy-eye, encamped at Big Island Grove, on the same river. These Indians frequently visited the homes and business houses of the whites during the winter, always appearing on friendly terms; but the sound of the war-whoop called out all the savage instinct of the race, and they joined Inkpaduta, and were recognized as being among the most zealous in the attack.

CHAPTER 11

Attack on Springfield

While the events, just related, were transpiring, Inkpaduta's band, with booty and captives, were moving in a north-westerly direction, camping in the groves along the streams, and by small lakes; never stopping two nights at one place; feasting upon the provisions taken from their hapless victims; and hunting for human game, in any defenceless settler, or unwary traveller, who might be in the region. They were also negotiating with the Indians on the Des Moines River for an attack on Springfield.

On the 20th of March, two strange and suspicious looking Indians visited Wood's store and purchased a keg of powder, some shot, lead, baskets, beads, and other trinkets. Each of them had a double-barrelled gun, a tomahawk, and a knife; and one, a very tall Indian, was painted black—so said one who saw them. They appeared sullen and not inclined to talk much, but said there were twenty lodges of them, all of whom would be at Springfield in ten days. Soon afterward, Black Buffalo, one of the Springfield Indians, said to the whites that the Indians who were at the store told his squaw that they had killed all the people at Spirit Lake. Just before the attack was made, these nominally friendly Indians suddenly, between two days, decamped for parts unknown, which looked suspicious. They told the whites, however, that Inkpaduta's band had started for the Big Sioux, and that there was no danger from them. This shows how much an Indian can be trusted.

When we encamped at Heron Lake, fifteen miles from Springfield, on the 26th of March, the warriors painted themselves in their most fierce and hideous fashion, and rifle in hand and scalping knife in belt, again sallied forth on the war-path, leaving us captives in charge of one of the warriors and the squaws. Before leaving, they took special pains to communicate to us by signs and gesture, and their jargon, the terrible work they meant to do. Knowing, as I did, that my sister was among their intended victims, and thinking that she would either be killed, or share with me what I felt to be a worse fate—that of a captive,—the anxiety I felt for her, and the rest of the people at Springfield, baffles description; but I could only await in suspense for their return.

From the time of the arrival of Mr. Markham, at Springfield, the people who gathered at the house of Mr. Thomas were living in hourly expectation of an attack. Twenty-one persons were packed in the rooms of this double-log house scarcely daring to venture outside the door, day or night. The fear and excitement that reigned within may be imagined from the fact, that one of the inmates (Mrs. Stewart) broke down completely, becoming insane. She had to be removed to her own home; her husband and three small children accompanying her.

As seventeen days had then passed, and no attack had been made; and as the soldiers from Fort Ridgley were daily expected; the people became inspired with the thought that there was no longer any danger. Accordingly they began to venture out.

The supply of fuel for the little temporary fort became exhausted, and must be replenished; hence, on Thursday morning, March 26, every man in the house turned out to chop and haul wood, continuing the work till afternoon, when they came in for dinner. For once, at least, Providence favoured the whites. Had the attack been made, even an hour earlier, while the men were out, the result must have been far more disastrous; and probably not a single person would have escaped.

About half past two or three o'clock, the eight-year old boy of Mr. Thomas, who was out playing in the yard, gave the alarm, by saying that Henry was coming. All the people, except Mrs. Church and Mrs. Thomas, were in the room on the north side of the house, the door of which opened toward the timber. As they were hourly expecting the return of the two men who had been sent to Fort Ridgley; and as they could not see any one coming from this direction without going out of doors, they all rushed out, expecting to see Henry Trets and Mr. Chiffen coming with the soldiers. But no such good news awaited them! Someone who was ahead of the rest saw an Indian dressed in citizens' clothing. Carver exclaimed, "Yes, it's Henry!"

But the next instant a number of guns cracked, and a volley of shot came from the rifles of the Indians, who were hid behind the trees, and the stable a few rods distant, and went whizzing among them. "The noble red man"(?)had used stratagem to draw the whites from the house, that they might shoot them down, when they were unarmed and unawares. The ruse well nigh proved successful. Little Willie Thomas, who had so innocently decoyed the people from the house, fell mortally wounded in the head. Three others—two men and one woman—were seriously though not fatally wounded. They all fled precipitately into the house, not even the wounded being aware that they were hurt.

Mr. Thomas was shot through the wrist, which eventually caused the amputation of his arm; David Carver through the inside of his left arm, the ball entering his side, from which it was never extracted; Miss Drusilla Swanger through the right shoulder, the ball striking the bone and coming out in front; and she had other slight flesh wounds.

It will be seen that the Indians had completely surprised and confused the settlers; but every man and woman knew full well that to be taken was certain death to all within the little fort, by the most horrible tortures that savages could devise; and each one was promptly at his post. There were only three men left unhurt: Jereb Palmer, (now residing near the scene of the conflict, [as at time of first publication]) Mr. Bradshaw, and Mr. Markham. Having a number of guns already loaded, Markham and Bradshaw seized them, and commenced firing in rapid succession, through the only port-hole there was on that side of the cabin. Mr. Palmer, assisted by Mrs. Thomas, promptly proceeded to barricade the doors and windows, and make port-holes, by taking out pieces of chinking from between the logs. Mr. Carver, in the excitement did not realize that he was wounded until he raised his gun to shoot, when he found that he had no control of his left arm. He was also seriously wounded in the left side.

The house being situated in the edge of a grove, the trees, together with the stable and underbrush, furnished abundant cover for the assailants; who kept up a constant firing upon every apparently vulnerable point. The besieged had to take up a portion of the puncheon floor, to put against the door, to protect themselves from the shower of bullets that found their way in. The fire was briskly returned by the three men, assisted by my sister and Miss Swanger, who rendered efficient service during the siege by casting bullets. Mrs. Louisa Church not only assisted by loading guns, but she actually fought as bravely as the men; shooting, through a port-hole, at an Indian who ventured out a little from his hiding place behind a tree.

When she fired, the Indian was seen to fall by others besides herself; but whether he was killed, or even wounded, no one ever knew for certain. If he was hurt, he was undoubtedly one of the Springfield Indians, as all of Inkpaduta's band returned safe to their camp. While some of the women were thus engaged, one, who had less courage than they, declared that she could not use firearms, but could pray. So in earnest supplication she implored help of Him who is able to save, or to destroy, both soul and body.

When the Indians fired on the whites, and the rush was made into the house, it was not noticed that Willie Thomas was missing. But when it was ascertained, by his mother that his body lay outside the door, writhing in agony from the fatal bullet of the savage, what wonder if, almost crazed with wrath,

Then flashed the living lightning from her eye,
And screams of horror rent the affrighted skies;
Not louder shrieks to pitying Heaven are cast
When husband or dear infant breathe their last.

She was deprived of the consolation of going out to smooth his brow and give one loving caress; or of having his body brought into the house, as it would have been certain death to venture out to get it. Her husband was also seriously wounded, and was bleeding profusely, while the awful work of death was going on without. How deep and manifold was the anguish endured by this poor woman.

The assault was vigorously kept up, and as vigorously resisted, till nearly sunset, when the Indians became weary of firing at blank walls, and being ignorant of the number of the inmates had not the courage to charge on the works; and doubtless, also impatient to engage in the work of plundering the vacated dwellings, abandoned the attack. Soon after the firing was discontinued, it was noticed that the Indians were throwing clubs at the horses, which were running loose around the stable, so as to drive them beyond gunshot of the house, in order to catch them and take them away without endangering their own lives.

All that day the work of death and plunder went on. At the house of Mr. Stewart, and at the store-house of Wood brothers, the attacks were more successful than upon the residence of Mr. Thomas. The confidence of William Wood in the friendship of the Indians proved altogether a delusion. They did not spare him any more than the rest. He was one of the first who fell. His charred and blackened remains subsequently found told the sad story of his awful death. It appears that after he was killed, or at least disabled, the Indians heaped brush upon his body, and set fire to it. His brother George, had evidently attempted to escape, but was overtaken by the Indians in the woods, shot down, and brush also was found piled upon his body.

An Indian well known to the settlers, who had always professed to be friendly, went to the house of Mr. Stewart, and pretended to want to buy a hog. Mr. Stewart started to go with him to the pen, when concealed Indians fired on him, killing him instantly. His poor wife was the next victim to their vengeance. With screams of fright she ran out of the house, and was brutally murdered, while stooping over the body of her dying husband with her babe clasped in her arms. The two remaining children ran out of doors, but while the Indians were killing Mrs. Stewart and the two younger children, Johnnie, the eldest, who was about eight years old, fled in fear and terror from the scene, and hid behind a log, where he remained concealed until the Indians left. At length he cautiously ventured from his hiding-place, and made his way to the cabin of Mr. Wheeler.

On reaching there he heard voices within, and in his frightened condition he supposed the people were killed, and the house was filled with Indians. He then started off through the woods toward the cabin of Mr. Thomas, where the murderous Sioux had just been. In doing so, he was in great danger from the Indians, and also from the whites, who, when they first discovered him approaching, mistook him for an Indian, in citizens' apparel, creeping along the ground. It being too dark for those inside to tell friend from foe at a distance, the men seized their guns, and in breathless silence waited to shoot him, as soon as he came within gunshot. But as he advanced the fact was discovered that it was no other than little Johnnie Stewart, which sent a thrill of pleasure to every heart.

This account was gathered from the testimony of the little boy himself. The seemingly miraculous escape of this child from the keen-eyed savages, by whose hands he was doomed to a life of cheerless orphanage, is indeed a wonder to all who hear of it. Subsequently he fell into the hands of Major Williams, whose kind and generous heart was touched with sympathy for the little orphan. He took him to his own home in Fort Dodge, where he resided for a number of years; and where I saw him upon my return from captivity.

Shortly after the firing ceased, a man of the name of Shiegley was seen going by the Thomas house, on his way to the cabin of Mr.

Wheeler, where his little boy was staying. They called to him through the port-holes, and he came to the house and was taken in. The Indians had not been to his cabin; consequently he had no knowledge of the attack. But he had heard the reports of guns about ten o'clock, in the direction of Wood's store. The fact that Mr. Shiegley and the Stewart boy had succeeded in entering the house without being molested encouraged the belief that the Indians had left the place.

THE FLIGHT

A consultation was then held, to decide what was the best course to take. From what had been ascertained, those at the Thomas cabin inferred that they were the only whites left in the settlement; and that their case was well-nigh hopeless, and began to canvass the subject of flight. But whither should they go, or how? The chances of escape were sadly against them, even if they made the attempt. It was a long distance to any point where they would be secure; the snow was still deep; the weather intensely cold; and the Indians had taken all the horses. Some of them were in favour of remaining, until help came, inside the sturdy walls of the old cabin, which had protected them so faithfully. Even though they remained, it was uncertain whether relief would ever come. They had no assurance that the messengers sent to Fort Ridgley had succeeded in reaching their destination; or whether their statement would be believed, and soldiers sent, if they had reached there. Moreover they did not know that the news of the outbreak had been carried to Fort Dodge; so did not expect help from there. Their greatest fear was, that the Indians would creep upon them, under cover of night, and set fire to the building; and that an escape from such an attack would be impossible.

About 9 o'clock, everything being quiet without—even the dogs, which seemed to comprehend the terrible calamity, having ceased barking—it was decided to leave the place. Anything but death at the hands of the merciless savages, even to perish on the open prairie, seemed preferable.

From what they knew of the character of the enemy, they had reason to suspect their silence was only a scheme to draw them out. Naturally, no one wished to be the first to venture outside the door, where little Willie's body lay cold in death, a sad reminder of the consequences of a former venture. But someone must be the first. So with true heroic courage, characteristic of the man, Mr. Markham volunteered to go to the stable, where the murderous Sioux had so lately been, and where they were perhaps secreted, and hitch the oxen to the sled and bring them to the door; while the others made hasty preparations for flight. So alone in the darkness he sallied forth, over the bloodstained snow, carrying his gun, to fire as a signal, should he find the enemy there, groped his way through the stable, silently brought out the patient oxen, put on the yoke, hitched them to the sled, and drove up to the door. There were still left seventeen persons, men, women, and children, three of them wounded; and all the conveyance they had was this one ox-sled. Hastily, but quietly, putting in the two wounded men and the smaller children, taking no baggage, and no clothing, except what they had on; even leaving the body of little Willie where he fell, they sadly and silently started on their journey down the valley of the Des Moines.

Something of the tediousness and painfulness of the journey, and the magnitude of the undertaking, may be judged from the fact, that by travelling as far as they could that night, and until sundown next day, they made only fifteen miles. At this distance they reached the cabin of George Granger, on the Des Moines, where is now the town of Estherville.

The night was cold, dark, and foggy, and the frightened and wounded fugitives slowly and painfully travelled on through the deep snow for several miles; when they became satisfied that they were deviating from the right course. The weary oxen were then unhitched, and turned out, to lie down; while the poor sleepless wanderers passed the remainder of the night out in the cold, watching for the savages. With the early dawn, they were again upon the move, continuing their weary march in the direction of George Granger's, until their oxen became entirely exhausted, when one of the party went on to get Mr. Granger to come for them with his team.

In the meantime, the fugitives left their oxen and sled, as preferable to waiting out on the prairie, stuck in a bank of snow, and were making their way, on foot, wounded and all, as best they could, when they were met by Mr. Granger and Mr. Palmer, the messenger sent to his cabin. About this juncture of affairs, they saw a man running at full speed across the prairie toward Granger's timber, who mistook them for Indians, and was so frightened that he pulled off his boots and threw them away, so as to run faster. When hailed by Mr. Palmer, intent only on saving his life if possible, he exclaimed: "*Ho!*" in the language and friendly salutation of the Sioux. It was then known to be the voice of Dr. Strong, who had left the Thomas cabin, before the attack, going to their neighbours, to see Smith and Henderson, who had lost their limbs by freezing. As Mr. Granger had come with only his oxen, intending to hitch them to the sled, which had been abandoned, the fugitives were still compelled to go on foot to his house.

On the same day, after being joined by Strong, they were overtaken by several other persons, who had been assailed by the Indians, and after being deserted by Strong decided to make their own escape.

After being handsomely repulsed by the heroic little band at the house of Mr. Thomas, the braves (?), who have long been celebrated and their names made famous by sickly sentimentalists, completely failed to muster sufficient courage even to enter the Wheeler house, under the guise of friendship. So they fired a few shots as they passed by, killing an ox which stood near the corner of the house. Some of the bullets passed through the door and on into the wall, barely missing Henderson, who was sitting on the bed. The only attempt made here to repulse the Indians was done by ringing bells and drumming on tin-pans; but this, it appears, was sufficient to frighten the brave warriors, as they abandoned the attack, and left the neighbourhood.

The next morning Dr. Strong, not having courage to return to the Thomas cabin, where he had left his family, persuaded Mrs. Smith to go and see if they were killed, which she did. Upon reaching there she found the house still as the grave, and saw the dead body of Willie Thomas lying out in the yard. She looked in the door and saw the floor was torn up, and blood spilt upon the floor and ground. Everything showed that a conflict had taken place. Her nerves not. being strong enough for the task of entering the house, she hurried home with the news of what she saw. Whereupon Dr. Strong left the place without making further investigation. He fled for dear life, as previously stated, without actually knowing the fate of his family. The varied emotions that struggled for utterance in the bosoms of these panic-stricken people, with whom life was far more important than their dead, or even the living whom they left behind in their flight, cannot be, even faintly, set forth in words. A fit opportunity was this to test poor human nature, which we must confess, when weighed, has sometimes been found wanting.

To cap the climax of woes: shortly after Dr. Strong left his neighbours in the Wheeler cabin, they likewise concluded to flee; leaving poor Henderson, who had both legs off, behind. Mr. Smith, who had lost only one leg, attempted to accompany the fleeing party; which consisted of his wife, Mr. Skinner and wife, Mrs. Nelson and child, about a year and a half old, and the little boy of Mr. Shiegley's; but after going a short distance he was compelled to give up the journey, by reason of his bleeding wound. Seeing he was unable to travel, Mrs. Smith[1] and the others abandoned him and Mr. Shiegley's little boy, on the prairie, where no white man could offer assistance or administer consolation. Thus he was left to crawl on his hands, or hobble along, and drag his torn and bleeding limb to the cabin. Who will say while gazing on this sad picture, that pen can portray it, or the imagination of man colour it at all equal to the dreadful reality?

When Mr. Shiegley heard that his boy was alive, and had been abandoned on the prairie with Mr. Smith, he expressed his determination to turn back in search of him; and turn back he did, in spite of the entreaties of the entire party, who hardly expected ever again to see him alive. He returned the next day, but was unable to find his boy, or Mr. Smith. He visited the cabin where Mr. Henderson was left, and cut a piece of meat from the ox, that had been killed by the Indians, and carried it in for the poor fellow to eat.

After refreshing themselves, and their worn animals, two nights and one day, at Mr. Granger's, and waiting the return of Mr. Shiegley, the entire party again proceeded on their journey. With fatigue and suffering, they travelled all day, and at night lay down without tents, or shelter of any kind. The wounds of those shot by the Indians had not been dressed, and, inflammation having set in, every motion caused excruciating pain.

With a bullet-wound in her shoulder, Miss Swanger walked for days, not over a smooth road, but across the trackless prairie, covered with snow, and wading sloughs and streams. A case of equal suffering, and equal endurance, is seldom found on record. She gradually recovered, however, from the effects of her wound, and is now the respected wife of Mr. W. J. Gillespie, of Webster City, Iowa.

Monday, the thirtieth, about 3 p. m., they were met by a company of volunteers from Fort Dodge, coming to their rescue. The joy of the weary, bleeding fugitives was indescribable on meeting the volunteers. Not until now had they for a moment felt safe from their foes, who, had they pursued them, would have found an easy prey. Especially was this a glad meeting for Mrs. Church, who among the volunteers recognized her husband, who had left his home on the nineteenth of November for Fort Dodge, and owing to the deep snow had not

1. Mrs. Smith returned to her husband, when met by the volunteers from Fort Dodge, and Mr. Henderson afterward went east to his friends.

returned.

Among the volunteers were Messrs. C. C. Carpenter (since governor of the state), J. F. Duncombe (now a prominent attorney), A. McBane (now president of the Merchants' National Bank), and C. B. Richards, all of whom were at the time, and are at this writing, residing at Fort Dodge, (as at time of first publication).

In the company were also K. A. Smith, now superintendent of public schools in Dickinson County; Captain W. V. Lucas, now of Chamberlain, D. T. (late state auditor of Iowa); W. R. Wilson (now deceased), who afterward married my sister, who was one of the refugees; T. M. Thatcher, whose wife was then a captive; and many others, as brave and noble men as ever went to the rescue of suffering humanity.

The injuries of those who were wounded by the Indians were carefully dressed by Dr. Bissell, the skilful surgeon of the expedition. The volunteers divided with them their provisions and blankets, and camped with them that night. The frightened women and children breathed free again, and slept in comparative safety. The next, day they were sent, under an escort, to the Irish settlement. In the course of time the fugitives reached Fort Dodge in a forlorn and destitute condition.

The property and household goods of all these people, including personal clothing, were either destroyed or carried off by the Indians. A large portion of the country was for a time deserted by settlers. Very few of the survivors of the massacre dared to return to their ruined homes, and most of them were destitute of means to return, if they desired to do so.

Note. This chapter is given upon the authority of Mr. Palmer, Mr. Markham, Mrs. Gillespie, Mrs. Church, and my sister.

Chapter 12

Official Account of the Massacre

The following is a copy of the official report of Major Williams, commander of the Spirit Lake Expedition.

Fort Dodge, Iowa, April 12, 1857.

To his Excellency James W. Grimes, Governor of the State of Iowa:

Sir:—Being called upon by the frontier settlers for aid in checking the horrible outrages committed upon the citizens living on the Little Sioux River, in Clay County, in the Spirit Lake settlements, and in Emmet County by the Sioux Indians, by authority you vested in me, I raised and organized and armed three companies of 30 men each, which were as we proceeded increased to over 37 men each. We took up our line of march on the 25th of March, and proceeded up the west branch of the Des Moines River to intercept the savages, who, reports said, were about to sweep all the settlements on that river.

By forced marches through snow-banks from fifteen to twenty feet deep, and swollen streams, we forced our way up to the state line, where we learned the Indians embodied 200 or 300 strong at Spirit Lake and Big Island Groves. Never was harder service rendered by anybody of men than by those 110 men under my command. We had to ford streams breast deep every few miles, and at all snow-banks or drifts had to shovel roads and draw our wagons through by hand with tug ropes, also the oxen and horses. All were wet all day up to the middle at least, and lay out upon the open prairies at night without tents or other covering than a blanket or buffalo-robe.

About 80 miles up we met those who had escaped the massacre at Springfield, composed of three men unhurt and two wounded, and one female wounded, and several women and children, in all numbering some 15 or 20 persons. They escaped in the night, carrying nothing with them but what they had on when they were attacked—had nothing to eat for two days and one night. They were about exhausted and the Indians on their trail pursuing them. Had not our scouts discovered them and reported, there can be no doubt that they would have been murdered that night. We found them in a miserable condition, destitute of everything, three of them badly wounded and several of the women without bonnets or shoes. They had nothing on them but what they had the night they fled; the poor women wading breast deep through snow and water, and carrying their crying children.

We halted at a small lake that furnished sufficient timber to make fires and warm them, furnished them with provisions, and gave them blankets to shield them from the severe weather, and gave them all the relief in our power. Our surgeon dressed the wounds of the wounded, whose wounds were in a bad condition. We encamped there with them that night, posting sentinels and pickets, expecting to be attacked. Next morning we sent them on with our scout to what is known as the Irish settlement, to remain until we returned, the settlers above that point having abandoned their homes and embodied themselves at that place where they were engaged in building a block-house. We proceeded on our march, throwing out in advance some 30 scouts, reconnoitring and examining every point where the enemy might possibly be found.

Every point of timber, lake, and stream was closely examined, and we found very fresh traces of the Indians throughout the day. From these tracks and trails they had all taken their course for Spirit Lake, or in that direction. By forced marches we reached the state line, near Springfield, and encamped about sundown on the margin of a grove; detailed 60 men armed, with rifles and six-shooters, with orders to cook their suppers and supply themselves with cold rations, each company their own, and be ready to march all night, in two divisions of 30 men each, and surprise the Indians before daylight next morning; furnished them with guides, as the information we had just received was that the Indians were embodied at or near the trading-house of a half breed by the name of Gaboo. We proceeded with great hopes of overtaking and giving a good account of them; but to our great mortification we found that they had all fled at the approach of 50 regulars from Fort Ridgley. Wood and Gaboo, traders, gave them the information that the troops were coming, and whose movements they sent their runners to watch. Had they not sent to Ridgley for troops, we would most certainly have overtaken them.

The conduct of the troops from Fort Ridgley is hard to be accounted for. On Thursday, the 26th of March, the Indians attacked Springfield and neighbourhood, The citizens defended themselves as well as they could. The battle and pillaging lasted until nightfall, when the Indians withdrew. On Friday, in the afternoon, the troops from Fort Ridgley arrived all well mounted on mules. Those troops lay at Springfield all day Saturday, and assisted in burying the dead. Their officers counselled with the half-breed Gaboo, who was the only one unharmed, and known to be acting with, and identified with, the Indians, and whose squaw (he is married to a squaw,) was at the time wearing the shawl of Mrs. Church, with other articles taken from the citizens. Said officers lay over from Friday evening till Sunday morning without pursuing or making any effort to overtake the Indians, who, they must have known, had taken off four white women as prisoners.

On Sunday morning he, the commanding officer, set out on their trail, and followed them half the day, finding their campfires, overtaking three or four straggling squaws, let them go, and finding all sorts of goods thrown and strewn along their trail to lighten their load and expedite their flight. When he could not have been over half a day's march from them, he stopped and returned the same evening (Sunday) to Springfield. When he ordered the men to return, they expressed a wish to follow on, and said they would put up with half rations if he would allow it. His reply was that he had no orders to follow them.

On Monday he set out for Spirit Lake to bury the dead, etc. He went to the first house, that of Mr. Marble, found one dead body, buried it, and returned to Springfield.

It is certain such troops, or rather such officers, will afford no protection to our troubled frontier settlers. Think of his conduct! his men, all well mounted, turning back when he was not a half day's march off them; they loaded down with plunder, and horses, and mules, and carrying off with them four respectable women as prisoners. The Indians were known to have twenty-five or thirty head of horses, and eight or ten mules, taken from the settlers. These Indians commenced low down on the Little Sioux River, near the southwest corner of Buena Vista County, and proceeded to break up and destroy all the settlements in the county, Clay, Dickinson, and Emmet Counties; then intended coming down the West Branch as far as they dare.

Throughout their whole course, they have completely demolished every settlement, killed all the cattle, ravished the women, and most scandalously abused them. They stood over the men with their guns cocked, while they were engaged in their hellish outrages. Along that river they approached, and got into, the houses through professions of friendship, and with a rush seized the men and arms, taking the people by surprise, attacking in such a way that one family could not help the other; all attacked simultaneously, robbed them of everything, in the midst of cold weather and deep snows. They did not commence to kill the settlers till they reached Dickinson County.

There, at Spirit Lake, it appears that the settlers had prepared to defend themselves, as well as they could, and from all appearances they fought bravely for their families. The settlers of Spirit Lake numbered over forty souls, not one of whom is left to tell the tale. Finding that the troops from Fort Ridgley had not buried the dead, I detailed twenty-five men to proceed twelve miles to the lake, and reconnoitre that district, and if no Indians were discovered to inter the dead as an act of humanity. Guides were procured, and they set out under the command of Captain Johnson and Lieutenant Maxwell, of Company C. They could find no Indians, but found their encampment, and a dreadful destruction of property. They performed the sad duty of interring the dead so far as they could find any.

They found and buried twenty-nine bodies, and found the skulls and bones of those who were burned in the ruins of a house, which, with one buried by the troops from Ridgley, made in all thirty-two dead found at Spirit Lake, seven killed at Springfield, and twelve missing at the lakes, certainly killed. It is supposed they are lying off at a distance, killed in attempting to escape. Some two or three were found who had been shot in attempting to escape, four of their women taken off as prisoners, and three badly wounded. I may sum up as follows: In all, 41 killed; 12 missing, no doubt killed; 3 badly wounded, two I fear mortally; 4 women prisoners. Besides several men from Boone River and counties east of this, who crossed the Des Monies River with a view of going to Dickinson County and the lakes, have never yet been heard from—supposed to be killed on their way.

From all appearances the Sioux Indians have determined to wage a war of extermination on our frontiers, as everything goes to show it at every point on the upper Des Moines, Big Island Grove, Spirit Lake, and all points where we found traces of them. They had left the most threatening signs, stakes set up and painted red, trees barked and painted, representing men pierced with arrows, etc. At every point they broke up and destroyed all furniture, burned the houses, and killed the cattle. Over 100 head of fine cattle were found shot down and untouched in any way but knocking off the horns—I suppose to make powder-horns. Their whole course goes to show that they intend to break up and stop the settlement of that north and northwest country.

Too much praise cannot be bestowed on the men I have had under my command on this occasion. Officers and men, without exception, have done their duty. They endured the greatest privations and fatigue without a murmur. For seventeen days they pressed forward on their march, waded rivers and creeks breast deep, and tugging wagons through snow-banks, sleeping on the prairies, frequently in their wet clothes, expecting every mile, after reaching thirty miles, to meet the Indians, as their threat was at Sioux River that they would sweep the Des Moines River settlements. Our men suffered very much, owing to the severe change and snowstorm. We have fourteen men badly frozen, and two lost, Captain Johnson, of Webster City, and Mr. Burkholder of this place, both frozen to death in a snowstorm. They were separated in returning from the lake. From the state of the men who succeeded in getting back to camp, both of these men must be dead. Every search has been made for them, but no discovery as yet. So severe was the weather that those who were picked up and got in were so much frozen and exhausted that they were crawling on their hands and knees when found, and three or four of them had lost their minds, becoming perfectly deranged, and knew no one.

As near as I could ascertain, the Indian force was from 150 to 200 warriors, judging from their encampments, etc. The number of Indians must be 15 or 20 killed and wounded. From the number seen to fall killed, and judging from the bloody clothes and clots of blood in their encampments, the struggle at the lakes must have been very severe, particularly the one at the house of Esq. Mattock. Eleven dead bodies were found at this house, together with several broken guns. They appear to have fought hand to hand.

I have to inform your Excellency that we have driven out of the north part of the state every Indian, and can say that at present there are no Sioux in the state, unless it be in that part near the mouth of the Big Sioux. The whole body have fled in the direction of the Missouri, crossing the Big Sioux. I shall not be surprised to hear of an attack on Sioux City. I am satisfied that the greater number of these Indians were from the Missouri, as they were strangers to the settlers where they appeared, and a portion of them were half-breeds. Never in the history of our country have such outrageous acts been committed on any people. We have no accounts of Indians committing such outrages on females as they have done—no doubt committed by the half-breeds. We have a host of destitute and wounded persons thrown upon us to provide for, both from Little Sioux River and the upper Des Moines River, as well as our own frozen and disabled men.

I forward this hasty and somewhat confused report; will give another soon, more in detail. I instructed Captain Richards, Mr. Morrison, and others to forward to you the affidavits, etc., to apprise you of our marching to relieve the frontiers, etc. Very respectfully yours,

W. Williams.

The following is an extract from Governor Grimes's message to the seventh General Assembly, January 12, 1858:

During the past three years my attention has been frequently called to the probability of a collision between the Indians and the settlers in the west and north-western counties of the state. I have repeatedly addressed the president of the United States, the secretary of war, and the commissioners of Indian affairs, warning them of the apprehended danger, and urging that immediate steps be taken to remove the Indians beyond our limits.

Without any military organization in the state, and without any power to act, except in the event of an actual hostile invasion; residing remote from the scene of anticipated difficulty, and fearful that some exigency might arise that would require prompt and energetic action, in January, 1855, I requested Major Williams, of Fort Dodge, to assume a general charge of this subject, and authorized him, as far as I had power to do so, to act in my behalf, in any contingency that might arise in connection with the Indian?

In February List, Ink-pa-du-ta's band of Sioux Indians made a hostile incursion into the state, and perpetrated most horrible atrocities in Dickinson county. When intelligence of this event reached Fort Dodge,. Major Williams at once enrolled three companies of men under Captains Richards and Duncombe, of Webster County, and Captain Johnson, of Hamilton County, and proceeded to the scene of difficulty. These heroic men left their homes in the most inclement season of the year, and endured almost unheard of sufferings and privations; crossing swollen streams flooded with ice, and traversing uninhabited prairies in the most tempestuous weather, that they might save their fellow-creatures from a savage butchery, or rescue them from a captivity worse than death.

Two of their number, Captain J. C. Johnson, of Hamilton County, and William Burkholder, of Webster County, perished on the march. Others returned frozen and maimed. The expedition did not overtake the Indians; but they reached the scene of their barbarities, gave to the dead a Christian burial, and brought back with them two children, the sole survivors of the slaughtered settlement.

The men who thus gallantly and humanely periled their lives have received no compensation for the time employed in the expedition, or for their outfit. The federal government is in equity bound for their compensation. The Indian tribes are under its protection and control. It has allotted to each tribe a scope of country for its exclusive occupation. It has sold lands to settlers in this state with the understanding that these tribes shall be confined to their respective limits, and that the possession of the land purchased shall never be disturbed by the government, or those under its management. If the savages break over their bounds and inflict injury upon others, the government should respond to the parties injured for the damages sustained, and for the expenses incurred in protecting themselves against a repetition of the injury. To this end I recommend that a memorial be addressed to the congress of the United States.

But many of the members of Major Williams's command are unable to await the tardy action of congress, and I therefore advise that the state assume the payment, and reserve the same from any appropriation that may be made.

I submit to the general assembly whether some public recognition of the noble gallantry and untimely death of Messrs. Johnson and Burkholder is not alike due to their memory and to the gratitude of the state.

I do not anticipate any further trouble from the Indians. The rumours put afloat in regard to future difficulty can generally be traced to interested persons who seek by their circulation to accomplish some ulterior purpose. To be prepared for any such emergency, however, I have established a depot of arms and ammunition at Fort Dodge, and have procured a cannon, muskets, and ammunition for another depot in Dickinson County.

CHAPTER 13

Burial of the Dead

When the first intelligence of these depredations reached the people of Fort Dodge, they were loath to believe the report. Those who have lived in an Indian country are aware how such rumours frequently get into circulation; and how often they prove untrue. Two men living on the Des Moines carried the news to Fort Dodge, as they received it from Mr. Markham; but being strangers, and having their particulars second hand, very little credit was given to the story. However, this was soon confirmed by Messrs O. C. Howe, R. N. Wheelock, and B. F. Parmenter, who had visited the lakes in the fall previous, and had taken claims where the town of Spirit Lake now stands. They had returned to their homes in Jasper County to spend the winter, and were going out to the lakes for permanent settlement.

From Fort Dodge they travelled up the west side of the Des Moines River, while the party who first carried the news came down on the east side; consequently these gentlemen had no knowledge of what had transpired until they reached the lakes at midnight on the 15th of March. They went to Mr. Thatcher's cabin, then to Mr. Howe's; but to their horror and dismay they found only lifeless bodies to welcome them. They at once inferred that this was the work of the Indians, and hastened back to Fort Dodge, arriving there on the 22nd of the month. Being well known their story was received without question.

The direful news created intense feeling throughout the country and excited the wrath and sympathy of all who heard it. Flaming editorials, in many papers, spread the feeling far and wide; loud and moving was the demand for relief for the living, and vengeance on the murderers.

Three companies of volunteers from Fort Dodge, Webster City, and Homer, comprising thirty men each, were immediately organized, under the command of Major Williams, of Fort Dodge: Co. A, Captain C. B. Richards, of Fort Dodge; Co. B, Captain John F. Duncombe, also of Fort Dodge; Co. C, Captain C. Johnson, of Webster City. Their mission was to bury the dead, relieve the living if any could be found and if possible overtake and punish the savages.

The expedition left Fort Dodge on the 25th of March, and as it proceeded others joined it, until the number increased to one hundred and ten men. All day long the companies forced their way through deep snow, and at night, cold and exhausted, lay down to rest with no covering but their blankets.

The settlers between Fort Dodge and the scenes of the massacre became alarmed for their safety, and fled from their homes. Hence the country, through which the volunteers passed, was well-nigh deserted. They were so eager to reach the scenes of depredation, that they did not wait for tents, and other provisions necessary for a winter campaign; consequently, the hardships they endured, while out on this humane mission, were many and perilous. After struggling on six days, they met the refugees from Springfield, Minnesota, (referred to in a former chapter,) at a point since known as Camp Grove, about eight miles above Emmetsburg.

On their arrival at Mr. Granger's cabin, about twelve miles east of Spirit Lake and nine miles southeast of Springfield, they learned that the United States troops from Fort Ridgley were at Springfield.

So it was not deemed necessary that the whole force should go to the lakes, and Major Williams detailed twenty-five men, under command of Captain Johnson, to bury the dead. They reached the scene of the massacre on the evening of April 3rd; and the next day performed their sad duty of interring the dead. The bodies had lain nearly four weeks where they had fallen, under the murderous rifle and war-club of the savages.

No graveyard had been located, and even if there had been it would have been impossible to move the bodies any great distance; so they were buried where they had fallen, on their own premises. There was no lumber for coffins, nor tools for their construction; so all that could be done was to dig the graves, deposit the bodies, and cover them over with mother earth. My father, mother, brother, sister, nephew, and niece, six in number, were laid side by side, in one common grave, a few rods southeast of the house. The grave is now marked by a mound of stones, and an evergreen tree, which I have recently planted.

Those found on the premises of Mr. Mattock were also laid in one

71

grave, near the ruins of the house. Dr. Harriott's body was taken up the following summer, by his father—being identified by a ring which he had on his finger,—and buried in a metallic coffin, on his claim, about three-quarters of a mile southeast of Dixon's beach. His grave is marked by boulders, placed there by his father, and an evergreen tree, recently planted by the writer.[1]

Carl Granger was buried near his cabin, where he fell, a few rods southeast of the present residence of Milton Smith, and near the track of the C., M. & St. P. R. R.

Joel Howe's headless body was buried on the southeast side of East Okoboji, on one of the large, oval-shaped knolls which stand out so prominently, near the lake shore. This knoll has natural shrubbery, especially on its northern slope, and is a beautiful and picturesque spot. His family was buried near their dwelling not far from the southern extremity of Tusculum Grove.

The bodies of Messrs. Noble and Ryan were buried near the cabin where they were found covered with straw, which was partially consumed by fire. The two children were buried beneath the tree, against which their brains had been dashed out. The house still stands, and the stumps of the trees still mark the graves of the children, (as at time of first publication).

The bodies of Messrs. Luce and Clark were among the missing at the time; but they were found some time in June, to the south east of East Okoboji, near the outlet. The body of Mr. Clark was identified by a memorandum-book. I have been unable to ascertain their burial

---

1. Isaac H. Harriott was born September 24, 1833, in Boundbrook, Somerset County, New Jersey. He was the son of James and Ann Eliza Harriott, and with his parents moved to Illinois when five years old. In 1848 his parents became residents of St. Louis, Missouri, and in 1849 removed to Pekin, where Harry began, study with a view to the medical profession, and placing himself under the tutorship of Dr. Maws remained in his care about three years. He next became a resident of Atlanta, Ill., where he pursued the study of medicine under Dr. Taney, at the same time acting as clerk in a drug-store. From Atlanta he removed to St. Paul, Minn., and thence to Red Wing, where he pursued his professional labours for a time. In 1856, he came to Lake Okoboji, where he fondly hoped to spend many years under the fair, blue sky in this delightful region. It was here that I had the pleasure of his acquaintance; he was genial, kind, and intelligent; his pleasant face was the light of every circle or gathering on that rude frontier. He enjoyed the confidence and esteem of all who knew him, and yet he fell in the strength of his manhood by the hands of bloodthirsty monsters, whom he had never wronged in word or deed. He was a cousin of Hon. A. V. Stout, a member of the Eighteenth and Nineteenth general assemblies of Iowa, from Grundy County.

place, but suppose they were interred where they were found. An old settler in the neighbourhood tells me there were, and perhaps are yet, two grave-mounds to be seen at or near the spot.

Mr. Marble was buried by the United States soldiers from Fort Ridgley, who came over from Springfield as far as his place. His grave is only a few rods from the western shore of Spirit Lake, and in the grove that bears his name.

The bodies found and buried on the ground of Mr. Mattock were taken up, by the later inhabitants, and reinterred on a high rolling prairie, in a retired and picturesque spot, on the farm of Jas. Helms.

I have been thus concise in pointing out the graves of these brave pioneers, who fell victims to the vengeance of the savages, as a guide to the travellers and strangers who annually visit this beautiful locality.

The detachment of volunteers above spoken of spent nineteen days in accomplishing the object of their mission. They suffered very much from exposure and fatigue, yet they performed their duty manfully, without complaint. It is sad to think, after all their toils and privations, that two of their number perished: Captain Johnson and William Burkholder, both noble fellows. They separated from their companies because of disagreement as to the route to be taken on their return trip, and were frozen to death on the prairie. Fourteen others were so badly frozen that they did not recover for nearly a year, and some were maimed for life.

Much time was spent by the friends of the two missing men, searching for their bodies. But, strange to say, it was not until August, 1868, eleven years afterward, that their bones and guns were found in Pocahontas County, lying side by side, within sight of a settlement. The relics were gathered up, and brought to Fort Dodge, where one of the largest funerals ever held in the city demonstrated the respect and sympathy of the people. Mr. Burkholder was a Mason, and in compliance with his oft expressed wish his remains were interred by the Masonic order. He was a brother to the wife of Hon. Cyrus C. Carpenter.

CHAPTER 14

Spirit Lake Expedition

From an account of the expedition that was published in the Hamilton *Freeman*, August 20, 1857, from the pen of Mr. H. Hoover, one of the volunteers, we make the following extract:

Being ready armed and equipped, we left Webster City at one o'clock March 23rd, and arrived that evening at Fort Dodge, where we were received by a large and enthusiastic meeting of the citizens of that county, who were already organized under the respective command of Captains Charles B. Richards and John F. Buncombe, and known as companies A and B. It now remained for us to form Company C, which we did, by electing the following gentlemen our officers: J. C. Johnson captain, John N. Maxwell first lieutenant, F. R. Mason second lieutenant, H. Hoover orderly sergeant, A. N. Hathaway corporal.
Company A.—Captain C. B. Richards, Lieutenant F. A. Stratton, Sergeant L. K. Wright, Corporal Solon Mason.

Privates—William Burkholder, George W. Brazee, C. C. Carpenter, P. D. Crawford, J. Conrad, Henry Carse, —— Chatterdon, W. Defore, J. H. Dalley, William N. Ford, —— Faurey, —— Gales, A. Hood, O. C. Howe, Angus McBane, William McCauley, Mike Maher, —— Mahan, W. P. Pollock, F. B. Parmeter, L. B. Ridgeway, Winton Smith, R. A. Smith, G. P. Smith, George B. Sherman, O. S. Spencer, C. Stebbins, S. Vancleve, R. W. Wheelock, W. F. Porter, D. Westfield, and O. Okeson. The last named was honourably discharged on the fourth day from sickness.

Company B.—Captain John F. Buncombe, First Lieutenant James Linn, Second Lieutenant S. E. Stephens, Sergeant William K. Koons, Corporal Thomas Callagan.

Privates—Jesse Addington, A. E. Busere, Hiram Benjaman, D. H. Baker, Orlando Bice, R. Carter, A. F. Crouse, F. R. Carter, M. Cavenaugh, Jeremiah Evans, Orlando C. Howe, D. S. Howell, Albert Johnson, Robert McCormick, W, Serls, John White, William R. Wilson, Washington Williams, James Murray, Daniel Morrissey, G. F. McClure, A. H. Malcome, M. McCarty, John McFarlee, Guernsey Smith, B. F. Parmetter, T. M. Thatcher, R. Whitstone, John O'Laughlin. The last named of whom was honourably discharged from inability to proceed.

Company C.—Captain J. C. Johnson, First Lieutenant J. N. Maxwell, Second Lieutenant Frank Mason, Sergeant Harrison Hoover, Corporal A. N. Hathaway.

Privates—Sherman Cassaday, A. K. Tullis, Elias D. Kellogg, A. S. Leonard, John Gates, T. B. Bonebright, Alonzo Richardson, Michael Sweeney, J. Brainard, Humphrey Hillock, F. R. Moody, Wm. K. Laughlin, E. W. Gates, W. L. Church, Jared Palmer, J. C. Pemberton, Thomas Anderson, J. Griffith, John Nolan, James Hidkey, Patrick Conlan, John Erie, Patrick Stafford, Morris Markham, J. Griffith, J. Bradshaw.

George B. Sherman acting commissary, and Dr. C. R. Bissell surgeon.

We now numbered near a hundred strong, efficient men; but as we were principally young, and inexperienced in the art of war, it appeared necessary that we be enrolled under the command of a chief officer, whose age and experience might qualify him to assume the position. 'Old men for council and young men for war.' The veteran Major Wm. Williams was unanimously conceded to be the man. The Major, though afflicted with rheumatism, and the frosts of seventy winters whitening his brow, resolutely set forward at our head.

We left Fort Dodge March 24th; but owing to our baggage-wagons being detained we did not proceed far, but encamped at Beaver Creek. We now began to realize that we were soldiers, for our appetites (true to nature) admonished us that we must prepare something to sustain the inner man. To this end we built three large campfires, and began (to most of us) the novel procedure of preparing our own refreshments. It was quite amusing to see the boys mix up meal, bake slapjacks, fry meat, wash dishes, and act the housewife generally; but it is said *practice makes perfect*, and the truth of the adage was substantiated in the case under consideration, for before our return some of the boys became quite expert in the handicraft above mentioned. One of our lieutenants—a jolly good fellow by the way—averred that he could throw a 'griddle-cake' out of the roof of a log-cabin, which he temporarily occupied, and while it performed divers circumgyrations in midair, could run out and catch it, 't'other side up,' on the spider.

That night we were fortunate enough to secure a bed beside a haystack. In the morning, Wednesday, 25th, we resumed our march. The only incident of the day was the crossing of the east fork of the Des Moines. This was not attended with much difficulty, as the stream was not as yet much swollen. We encamped for the night at Dakota City.

Thursday, 26th. As we proceeded on our journey the trail became more and more obscure, and the snow apparently deeper. Some places the snow was so hard as to require breaking down before our teams could possibly pass. In other places it had drifted into the ravines to the depth of eight or ten feet. The water had drained off the prairies into these hollows, converting the snow into slush, and rendering it almost impossible to pass them.

Those of us who were 'green hands' had now an excellent opportunity of learning the definition of the term 'actual service;' for it soon became evident that the only practicable mode of proceeding was to wade through, stack arms, return and unhitch the teams, and attach ropes to them and draw them through. This done, we performed a similar operation on the wagons; then rigged up, broke roads to the next slough, and amused ourselves with a repetition of the aforesaid interesting performances. In this manner we were two days in reaching McKnight's Point, on the west bank of the Des Moines, twelve miles from Dakota City. In this region the snow was about two feet deep, hard on the top, and soft beneath: too weak to support the weight of a man, thus making the travelling very tiresome. Our guides had gone on ahead to select the most practicable route; they were followed by the 'foot,' and the rear was brought up by the baggage-wagons.

Under all this complication of difficulties, the conduct of our gallant commander, Major Williams, was deserving of the highest praise, and worthy of the emulation of those of greater physical strength and fewer years. He was always upon the alert, as from the reports we knew not what moment might find us in a savage ambuscade. Frequently he was on foot, wading through the ice and snow at the head of his men, by his voice and example cheering and inspiring them on their weary way, and proving himself alike entitled to the name of an experienced soldier and high toned gentleman.

It was Friday, the 27th, that we arrived at McKnight's Point. Here we found our guides, Captain Buncombe and Lieutenant Maxwell, who had succeeded, through almost superhuman exertions, in reaching the point the night before. Captain Buncombe suffered greatly from the severe labour and exposure of the trip, and was assisted to reach the settlement, where he arrived benumbed with cold and almost insensible. The next morning he was again on duty, and notwithstanding his recent exhaustion, and the advice of his friends to remain behind, like a true soldier resumed his command and nobly persevered in its toilsome labours.

On Saturday morning, the 28th, for reasons best known to themselves, some eight or nine of the party—I blush to relate it—came to the conclusion that a 'peep at the elephant' was sufficient, so they 'just naturally backed out,' and struck a 'bee-line' for home. The cause of this singular escapade was at the time a mystery to me, but the supposition was entertained that they believed *discretion to be the better part of valour.* I afterward learned the cause of their retreat. The romance of the affair had become worn off by contact with material things, and the mirage of glory was fast dissolving in the presence of the stern reality which was beginning to make itself visible in a tangible form. It was apparent that their military enthusiasm had become somewhat 'bleached out' by the exercises of the two previous days; 'going a soldiering' evidently was not in their line. We made no objection—thinking it better to let the 'chaff blow off.' Therefore, renewing our march, we reached the mouth of the Cylinder Creek that night.

Sunday, 29th. We reached the Irish colony, twelve miles above.

Here were a number of persons from a settlement in Minnesota, who had left their homes on account of the Indian troubles. These, together with other accessions, brought our number up to 125 strong.

Monday, 30th, left our teams, which were pretty much exhausted, and having supplied ourselves with fresh ones we proceeded onward. When about five or six miles from the settlement, our advanced guard met what they supposed to be Indians, but upon a nearer approach they proved to be a party of fugitive men, women, and children flying from the scene of bloodshed and butchery which they had just escaped.

Tuesday, the 31st, reached Big Island Grove, where we encamped to reconnoitre, as we expected to find the Indians in that vicinity. We were disappointed, although comparatively recent signs were visible. We found an ox which had been killed, his horns cut off, and the hide laid open along his back, a little innocent amusement of the savages. But 'nary red' skin was to be seen.

April 1st. This morning, when a short distance on our way, an amusing incident occurred. The Major had sent forward a party of scouts, with orders not to fire a gun unless they encountered Indians. Some of our party hearing the report of a gun, a halt was ordered, when all heard a number of shots in rapid succession, and directly a party of men was seen issuing from the grove in advance of us, as though they were pursued. The cry of 'Indians' was at once raised, and our men (exasperated by the recital of deeds of treachery and violence to which they had recently listened) became ungovernable, and rushing from their ranks threw themselves into defiant attitude. Some of them went so far as to cock their guns, although the 'enemy' were at least *two miles distant.*

However, the Major soon succeeded in restoring order, and convincing the 'fast young men' that their movemerits were somewhat premature. The supposed Indians proved to be our scouts who had encountered some otter on the lakes, and in pursuing them had become so excited as to entirely forget their orders, and hence firing of guns and the consequent excitement in the ranks.

Proceeding on our way we reached G. Granger's on the river near the Minnesota line. Here very unwelcome news awaited us. We learned that the Indians had left the place five days in advance of our arrival, and that a detachment of United States troops, sixty in number, were then quartered at Springfield. These tidings were particularly annoying to us at this juncture of affairs, and productive of considerable disappointment and vexation. We had hoped that, if we did not reach the scene of action in time to afford the distressed settlers relief, we might at least reach it in time to deal out justice to their murderers. After all our toil and privations, endured in hope of accomplishing something, to be informed that we were 'considerable behind time,' gave occasion to no very pleasant reflections.

Upon inquiring, we learned that the United States troops from Fort Ridgley had arrived the next day after the Indians had left, and that a few of them had followed the Indians a short distance, and discovered where they had encamped the night before, and from the number of their *teepes* computed them to number about forty warriors. On the way they found various articles of clothing and other materials cast away by the Indians on account of the great amount of plunder with which they were burdened. But those ferocious 'dogs of war,' after being set on a warm scent, and having their prey almost within their grasp, suffered them to escape unscathed.

Our position at this time was rather a perplexing one. Anticipated by the United States troops, the Indians five or six days in advance of us, and our provisions almost exhausted, it soon became apparent that the only alternative left was the painful one of abandoning the pursuit, paying the last tribute of respect to the remains of the unfortunate settlers, and returning home. Accordingly, on the morning of April 2nd, a company of twenty-five men were selected and placed under the command of Captain J. C. Johnson, with orders to proceed to Sprit Lake and bury the dead, while the residue were to return to the Irish colony. I was prevented from joining the company by an accident (a severe sprain of the ankle) which unfitted me for travelling. But the following are the most prominent particulars of their adventures, furnished me by a friend:

BURIAL OF THE DEAD.

Two of our number were mounted on horseback and carried provisions. On arriving at the river it was found that the horses could not be taken across, so the provision was distributed among us, and the horsemen returned. About 3 o'clock that day, we arrived at the house of Mr. Thatcher. The door being shut, we opened it and entered the house. Within we found everything in utter confusion. Hearing an exclamation of surprise outside, I went out and there beheld the bodies of two men lying side by side, brutally murdered by numerous shots in the breast (where the brave invariably receive the missiles of death). This sight convinced us that we had at least a painful duty to perform, if we did not encounter the infamous villains who perpetrated this cruel deed. We proceeded to bury them immediately. Our captain appointed two to dig the grave, while the remainder (except the guard) proceeded to the house of Mr. Howe, about a mile beyond.

Here the door was also closed; on opening it, a sight met our eyes which sent a shudder through our veins and fired our minds with thoughts of vengeance and dire retribution upon the cowardly assassins. It was such a sight as a sensitive person might well avoid encountering, and which for humanity's sake we would gladly have erased from our memories, but there it confronted us in all the tragic horror of a fearful reality. There lay before us, in an incongruous heap, the mangled forms of seven human beings, from the aged grandmother down to the prattling child of tender years, who alike fell victims to the merciless savages' inordinate thirst for human blood. After covering the bodies we returned to our companies and buried the two first found, also a little daughter of Mr. Thatcher.

Next morning returned, found another body a few rods from the house, and buried them all in one grave. We next proceeded to Granger's, about three miles distant. Here we found one man lying in front of the house brutally murdered, his face literally chopped to pieces, and several marks of a tomahawk in the breast; a large bulldog was lying by his side, which probably died in valiantly defending his master. This house was also completely ransacked, everything carried off that could possibly be of any value to the Indians.

We then visited the house of Mr. Mattock, about a half mile further on, just across an arm of the lake and situated in a grove of heavy timber. We found one man and three or four head of cattle lying on the ice. As soon as we entered the grove we could see the bodies of men, women, children, and cattle scattered promiscuously about and mutilated in the most shocking manner.

From all appearances here had been the struggle for life. Here was where the white and red man met in mortal combat and closed in the fearful death-struggle: the one for life, home, wife, and children, the dearest ties that bind souls to earth; the other to gratify the most fiendish passions which human nature in its most degraded and degenerate forms is heir to: revenge, malice, hatred, envy, and covetousness, and above all, an inherent "penchant" to signalize, themselves by imbuing their hands in the blood of the palefaces, irrespective of age, sex, or condition. The battle had evidently been fierce and hotly contested, but the whites, overpowered by numbers, sank like Leonidas's band, covered with wounds and heirs to immortal fame. The house was burnt, and in one corner the charred remains of a human body was found. Here we buried eleven. This was near the Indian camp.

At the house of Mr. Gardner we found six dead bodies, one in the house and the remainder just outside the door. We buried them all together about fifty yards from the house, on a spot designated by a daughter of Mr. Gardner, whom we met on our way up as a fugitive from Springfield. We buried twenty-nine in all. Several were missing, among whom were Mrs. Thatcher. Mrs. Marble, Mrs. Noble, and Miss Gardner, who were supposed to have been carried away captives by the Indians. Our melancholy task being done, we took supper and repaired to rest. Sleep coming to our aid we were soon oblivious of the past. In the morning we were very much refreshed, and taking a hasty meal of potatoes we bid *adieu* to Spirit Lake, the scene of this dreadful massacre, the thoughts of which filled our minds with an utter abhorrence of the whole Indian nation, and turned to join our companions in their homeward march.

April 3rd. Reached the Irish colony. The following morning, April 4th, was very disagreeable, rainy, and cold; but as our provisions were daily diminishing in quantity and deteriorating in quality it was deemed prudent to resume our march. About one o'clock we reached the banks of Cylinder Creek, which, owing to a recent rain and the melting of the snow, was impassable. This creek pursues a meandering course in a little valley of perhaps a half mile in width. The flats were entirely overflown with water about waist-deep; while in the channel or bed of the stream the water was eleven or twelve feet deep. A halt was ordered; which was a very judicious movement, seeing that we were unable to proceed any farther.

Some of our party constructed a boat out of a wagon-bed, no doubt with the laudable design of transporting us across the 'vasty deep;' but, alas for 'human foresight,' it served to carry over three persons, but refused to return for a second cargo; as the 'head wind' was by this time so strong as to resist all the endeavours of the experimenters to return. While awaiting the result I was irresistibly reminded of a certain couplet relating to the River Jordan: *Part have crossed the flood and part* (fain would be) *crossing now*, the only thing preventing being an entire absence of means; the doctrine that *the end justified the means*, being thereupon no consolation to them.

We now found ourselves in rather an unenviable situation, a prospect of drowning if we proceeded, a prospect of starving if we remained where we were, and ditto if we returned. Various plans were proposed only to be decided impracticable. However, it was determined that the teams should return to the settlement. Accordingly the Major with the wounded settlers and a few others returned. The balance of us concluded to provide for ourselves.

For my own part I confess to being no little puzzled to know how to dispose of myself. I knew that there was not provision enough at the colony for us all, and as to starving where I was, I looked upon the chance for life as being one to ten against that of freezing to death, as it was growing colder every moment and the wind blowing a hurricane. The only avenue open to me lay in the possibility of crossing the creek; but even of this *hope told no flattering tale.* Just then I remembered the words of Napoleon, when told by his engineers that the passage of the Alps was *bare-*

ly practicable, Set forward! Accompanied by a friend I ascended the steam about a mile, where I saw a bunch of willows; these I knew grew upon the bank of the channel and might perhaps assist us in crossing, if we were fortunate enough to reach the place. After wading about 80 rods we reached them, and found behind them what had been a snow drift, now a compound of snow and water denominated 'slush' and extending perhaps half way across the bed of the stream.

By breaking willow brush and covering it we made a partial bridge which served to support us as far as it went. The only alternative now was to jump, which I did, and to my surprise and gratification brought up in only five feet of water, having been lucky enough to reach the opposite bank of the channel. My comrade now threw our blankets and followed. By again wading some distance we gained the bluffs, thankful that the Rubicon was passed. By running four miles we reached a house where we obtained shelter for the night.

Sunday, April 4th. Returned to the creek to look for our companions. As there were no signs of life to be seen, the conviction forced itself upon us that our fears were realized and that they were all frozen to death. The stream was by this time all frozen over except the channel. Captain C. B. Richards in particular deserves praise for his noble efforts in behalf of the sufferers. He worked two hours in the severe cold, attempting to crawl over the ice to reach the shore; but notwithstanding the captain's warm heart the intense cold overcame him, and he was obliged to abandon his philanthropic project without accomplishing his object. In justice to him and Captain Duncombe, I must say that they did all that under such circumstances could be done to relieve their men. Some of us tried to break away across for the boat, but the effort proved futile and we were obliged to abandon the idea of reaching the place where we had left our companions, so we returned to the house to await further developments.

Monday, April 6th. Again proceeded to the creek and found the ice strong enough to carry a horse. Crossed over and with joy and surprise found our companions all alive. They were piled up like so many flour-bags 'in the most approved style,' under a tent constructed of a wagon-cover, and with a quantity of bedding which they fortunately had on hand were enabled to keep from freezing; and now they crossed on the ice, (which they had patiently awaited the formation of) after lying in this position over forty hours *without food or fire on the open prairie.*

But great as were their privations and sufferings, they were exceeded by those of our party who left Spirit Lake on Sunday to cross the prairie to the Irish settlement. They left Spirit Lake Saturday, April 4th, and travelled in a southeast direction, intending to reach, if possible, the Irish colony that day; but, owing to the many deep sloughs which they were obliged to cross, they failed in accomplishing their object. Towards evening their clothes began to freeze to their bodies and to impede their progress. Some of the party still continued to plunge in and wade through, while others deemed it prudent to evade them as much as possible in order to avoid having their clothes frozen, stiff upon them. The necessary consequence was, they became separated, some travelling in one direction, and some in another. The main body, however, with W. K. Laughlin as guide, kept a nearly direct course. Just before dark they passed a small lake skirted by a few trees. Some proposed to stop and pass the night, but the voice of the majority was in favour of travelling all night, to escape being frozen to death; but overtasked and exhausted nature will assert her rights.

About eight o'clock at night they were overcome by hunger, cold, and fatigue, and being unable to proceed any further lay down on the open prairie, exposed to the merciless wind which swept past like a tornado, their clothes frozen stiff as a coat of mail. Without food, fire, or protection of any kind, they spent a sleepless night. Sleep came and offered the tired wanderers relief, but it was the treacherous sleep of death. A few resigned themselves to its influence, but the more experienced knew it would be their 'last sleep' if they were permitted to indulge in that fatal stupor, the sure herald of *the sleep that knows no waking.* The grateful thanks of more than one of that forlorn company are due to John N. Maxwell and W. K. Laughlin for forcibly keeping them awake through the tedious watches of that awful night. In the morning they found themselves in sight of timber on the Des Moines River, and roused their last remaining energies to reach it. Those who had drawn off their boots were unable to get them on again so they were compelled to cut up their blankets and wrap their feet in them.

In this manner they reached the settlement on Sunday, April 5th, where they all ultimately arrived except two. These were Captain J. C. Johnson, of Webster City, and William Burkholder, of Fort Dodge. They were last seen about five o'clock Saturday, two miles distant from their companions, and travelling in a southerly direction. It was confidently hoped that they might have strayed down the river and found a lodging-place. Every effort was made to ascertain their whereabouts, but without success. Their comrades were at length forced to the conclusion that they had lost their way and had perished in attempting to reach the settlement. Their melancholy fate threw a gloom over the whole company, as they were special favourites. I was not personally acquainted with Burkholder, but had the honour of being a friend of the lamented Captain Johnson. As such I feel it my duty to offer, in my humble way, that tribute which is justly due to his memory.

John C. Johnson was born and raised in Westmoreland County, Pennsylvania. With a view of bettering his circumstances in life, he removed to Illinois, and subsequently to Hamilton County, Iowa, near Webster City. It was here I first got acquainted with him; his gentlemanly manners and generous, frank disposition winning my esteem and confidence. When the news of the Indian outrages reached us, his business claimed his attention at home; but unmindful of interests he thought only of the sufferings and wrongs of the unhappy victims, and knew no other way than that pointed out by duty and patriotism. On the morning of our departure he remarked to me that 'Pennsylvania's sons should not be weighed and found wanting,' and most nobly did he sustain his assertion throughout the arduous labours of the expedition.

So favourable was the impression made by him on the company that he was unanimously chosen our captain, and subsequently proved himself worthy of the confidence reposed in him. He faithfully fulfilled the orders of his superior officer, maintaining order and decorum in his company. His orders were given in a manner to insure promptness of execution, but yet in such a courteous and affable manner that it was a pleasure to obey him. He appeared to have the comfort and welfare of his company at heart, and by his noble, self-sacrificing nature won golden opinions from all who became acquainted with him. I marched beside him through the day, and slept beside him at night, and I must say I never met one to whom I became so much attached in so short a time; and I firmly believe I but reflect the sentiment of his company in saying that there was not one who did not esteem and love him.

But *Death loves a shining mark.* The good and gifted are not exempt from his power, but equally liable to be stricken down with the most delicate flower that hangs by a fragile stem exposed to the sweeping blast.

'Tis hard indeed to part with those
Whom we would have forever nigh,
But shall we murmur if God choose
To call their spirits to the sky?

Our only comfort is found in submission to the will of Him who doeth all things well.

Monday, April 6th. Those of us who had succeeded in crossing the Cylinder now thought best to reach home as soon as possible, as we were out of provisions altogether. After paying our bills *to the last farthing* where we stopped over Sunday, we departed 'every man to his tent' and arrived home in three or four days, weary, worn and wasted. We met with a hearty welcome from our friends, who were gratified to see us return alive. Although some of us were pretty badly frozen, we considered ourselves extremely fortunate in having escaped the fate of our comrades. Thus ended the disastrous Spirit Lake Expedition, a second edition (on a small scale) of Bonaparte's expedition *to Moscow.*

Recapitulation—All those engaged in the expedition arrived safely at home, except two above mentioned, of whom nothing, as yet, has been heard. Of the women taken prisoners, two, Mrs. Noble and Mrs. Thatcher, were murdered by the Indians; the others, Mrs. Marble and Miss Gardner, were ransomed. Two more bodies have since been found and buried at Spirit Lake. A town is now laid out where the massacre (equal to that of Wyoming) took place. It is fast settling with active and energetic men. It is situated in Dickinson County, 140 miles from here, and destined to become an important point in north-western Iowa."

CHAPTER 15

Return of Warriors

After an absence of two days, the warriors who had gone to the attack on Springfield returned to our camp, bringing in their plunder. They had twelve horses, heavily laden with dry goods, groceries, powder, lead, bed-quilts, wearing apparel, provisions, etc. They gave us to understand that they had met with a repulse; but to what extent we could only conjecture. They told us they had killed only one woman. Whether that was my sister or not, I could not tell.

Among this plunder were several bolts of calico and red flannel. Of these, especially the flannel, they were exceedingly proud; decorating themselves with it in fantastic fashion. Red leggings, red shirts, red blankets, and red in every conceivable way, was the style there, as long as it lasted. Could anything have amused me in those sad days, it would have been, to see their grotesque attempts to wear the habiliments of the whites; especially the attempts of the squaws to wear the tight-fitting garments of the white women. They would put in one arm, and then reach back to try to get in the other; but, even if they succeeded in getting both arms into the sleeves at the same time, they were too broad-shouldered, and brawny, to get the waist into position, or fasten it; so after struggling awhile they would give up in disgust. They were altogether too much the shape of a barrel, to wear the dresses of white women. So they cut off and threw away the waists, and made the skirts into loose fitting sacks after the squaw fashion. All this amused them, greatly; they would laugh and chatter like a lot of monkeys.

Early on the morning after the warriors returned from Springfield, they started for the unbroken wilderness of the northwest. A male Indian never does anything that can be called labour; it is against his principles, and would lower his dignity, work is only fit for women. Such is an Indian's sense of honour. The women are only slaves; and we, poor captives, were slaves of the slaves.

After the first day's ride, (to which I previously alluded,) I was compelled to trudge on foot; and given a pack to carry. This was from time to time increased, until I had not less than seventy pounds. I will give the contents of the pack (that the reader may judge of its weight): eight bars of lead, one pint of lead-balls, one *teepe* cover made of the heaviest, thickest cloth, one blanket, one bed-comforter, one iron bar, three feet long and half an inch thick, (the use of which I did not know,) one gun, and one piece of wood several inches wide and four feet long, to keep the pack in shape. This was bound together with ropes, and strapped on my back. The other captives fared no better, and if possible worse.

Mrs. Marble, besides a pack equally as heavy as my own, had to carry a great lubber of a *papoose*, nearly two years old. This was seated on the pack, inside the blanket, and when awake would stick up its head, over her shoulder, clasping its arms around her neck; but when asleep, it would sink into a heap, apparently heavier, and certainly more difficult to carry. At such times, watching her opportunity when the Indians were not looking, she would reach over her shoulder and claw him in the face; thus making him wake up, and as he could not talk he could not tell what was the matter. This made him cry, so that the squaws concluded: "*Papoose* no like white woman," and took him away. The only thing that ever amused me, during all the time I was with them, was seeing Mrs. Marble watching her opportunity, and clawing that filthy *papoose*. So interested in this did I become, that while walking by her side, in the rear of the train, I would watch the Indians, and tell her when to "go for" the *papoose*.

While we, poor captives, were trudging along through the deep snow, bearing our heavy burdens, the warriors were tripping over the drifts on snow-shoes, unencumbered. The squaws carried still greater loads, but they, too, had snow-shoes; while we sank beneath our burdens into the deep snow, frequently finding it almost impossible to wallow through.

These hardships, proved too much for Mrs. Thatcher whose babe had been torn from her bosom. Taking cold, as she inevitably must, she was thrown into phlebitis fever and a combination of ills, resulting in the most excruciating suffering. One breast gathered and broke, and one limb, being swollen to nearly twice its natural size, turned black, even to her body, and the veins were bursted by the pressure. No woman, in like condition at home, would think of being out of her bed; and would require both medical attendant and nurse, day and night; but she, poor woman, was compelled not only to tramp through the snow, and wade through ice-cold water, waist-deep, but even to chop and carry wood at night, and help to do other drudgery about the camp, such as cutting poles and dragging them in, putting up tents, and all such work.

This may seem like an exaggeration; but it is strictly true. I was an eye-witness. Language cannot express the sufferings she endured, or the fiendish barbarity of her heartless masters. When she could no longer move her limb, she was put on a horse for a few days; but this was only another method of torture; the wonder is, that she did not faint and fall from her horse. She bore up, through all her sufferings, with remarkable fortitude; hoping that the time might come when she should be rescued from her captors, and restored to her husband; for whom she manifested an attachment both heroic and sublime. Meantime their "medicine-man" took her in hand, and really gave her relief; but how much she gained by it the sequel will show.

The provisions taken from the whites lasted about four weeks; during which time they did no hunting, fishing, or anything to increase or eke out their store; nothing, in fact, but tramp, eat, and sleep. The Indians have no equal as gormandizers; they are perfectly devoid of anything like delicacy of appetite, or taste, or decency in the matter. Every part of an animal is devoured, cooked or raw, clean or unclean; the smaller game is sometimes roasted without opening; and if the entrails are taken out they are thrown on the fire and roasted, and eaten by the squaws, this being considered the right of the cook. Animals that have lain dead until putrescence has well begun are devoured with avidity. Fish found along the beach, that have lain till the flesh was actually dropping from the bone, were eaten without even being cooked, and pronounced: "*washta-do!*" (very good!) It was no unusual thing, indeed, to see the most delicate *belles* in Inkpaduta's train picking from the head of a *papoose* a vermin—such as Burns saw on the ladle's bonnet at church, and cracking them in her teeth.

They have no regularity about their meals. It is always dinner time if they have anything to eat. They will eat until they can eat no longer; and then lie down and grunt and puff, like cattle gorged with grass in the spring-time; or like overfed swine. Thus they will lie and sleep and snore for an hour or two; then get up and smoke, and eat again. This is especially the habit of the "gentlemen" of the party; the "ladies" contenting themselves with what their lords cannot eat, and resting their weary bodies by cutting wood and backing it up; or by preparing something more to please the taste of their "better halves."

The Indian is an inveterate smoker; and if he had whisky would go to the same extremes with that. They got a large quantity of tobacco from the whites, more especially at Springfield; but all this would not have lasted long, if they had not extended it by a free use of *kinnikinic*—a species of red willow that grows abundantly, on wet soil throughout the Northwest. They frequently 'smoke the leaves, but prefer the bark, which is much stronger. It acts as a narcotic. The squaws prepare the bark by scraping it off the twigs and drying it, in the winter by the fire, on a grate made of strips of bark, woven across a frame; and in summer on a piece of buckskin in the sun. We were frequently compelled to help prepare it.

Their lodges, or *teepes*, are conical tents, and vary in size from fourteen to twenty feet or more in diameter; they are made of the thickest, heaviest, kind of cloth, or skins, and kept in shape by *nine* poles. The fire is built in the centre, and the smoke escapes through an aperture at the top, made for that purpose. They make their beds of straw, mats, blankets, buffalo robes, etc. These they arrange around the fire; and on them they not only sleep, but eat, and sit to smoke through the day.

CHAPTER 16

The Indians Pursued

Scarce twenty-four hours had elapsed since the attack on Springfield, and much less than that from the sad flight of the fugitives, when a company of United States soldiers arrived from Fort Ridgley, under command of Captain Bee. They, too, like the volunteers from Fort Dodge, had endured almost incredible hardships, and surmounted every conceivable difficulty. They lay over one day at Springfield, and, although exhausted from the journey already taken, attempted the pursuit of the Indians. Twenty-four men, under Lieutenant Murray, came so near overtaking us that they reached at 3 p. m. the place left by us in the morning. When their presence was discovered by the Indians, the wildest excitement reigned among them. We were encamped on a low piece of ground by a small stream of water. Between us and the soldiers was a high, rolling prairie, so that the camp was not visible to the soldiers; but the Indians from the higher ground could see all the movements of their pursuers. Such was the situation, indeed, that the soldiers, had they followed on our trail, would not have discovered our presence until in our very midst.

The squaws at once extinguished the fires by pouring on water, that the smoke might not be seen; tore down the tents; packed their plunder; and with the wounded Indian, (the one shot by Dr. Harriott,) and a sick *papoose*, hastened from the camp down the creek, skulking like partridges among the willows. One of the Indians crept along the ground to the base of a tree, some rods from the camp, on higher ground, and perched himself among its branches. Here he could observe the movements of the soldiers, and report them to his comrades. The rest of the warriors, with ourselves, remained on the camp-ground. One Indian was detailed to stand guard over us, and to kill us if there was an attack. The rest of the warriors prepared for

91

battle.

First they discharged their guns into the earth, to empty them of the loads of shot they already contained; but so that the reports could not be heard any distance. Then they reloaded them with bullets. The excitement manifested by the Indians was for a little while intense; and although less manifested ours was fully as great, as we were well aware that the Indians meant all they said when they told us we were to be shot, in case of an attack. We therefore knew that an attack would be certain *death to us*, whatever the results might be in other respects.

After an hour and a half of this exciting suspense, in which the squaws were skulking in the willows; the sentry watching from the tree-top; the warriors lurking among the openings of the willows on the banks of the stream; and we cowering beneath the muzzles of the loaded rifles,—a sudden change came to us. The soldiers, it seems, just here decided to turn back. In conversation with both Captain Bee and Lieutenant Murray at Fort Ridgley, on my return from captivity, I learned that their guides (two half-breeds,) assured them the campfires were at least two or three days old; and hence their decision to relinquish the pursuit. It is easy to believe that the soldiers, having confidence in their guides, might have been misled by them; but guides worthy of the name should not have made such a mistake. It could not have been more than nine hours, after we left the grove, until the soldiers entered it.

Possibly, some pains had been taken to obliterate the traces of our encampment; but if such is the Indian custom the guides should have known it, and made allowance for it. At the time we were captured, our shoes were taken from us, and *moccasins* given us instead, that we might leave no evidence of our presence in the trail; but no reasonable guide would have declared that there were no whites in the company, because no *shoeprints* were seen. Lieutenant Murray informed me that at first they were so sure that we were in the grove, that they surrounded it, hoping thus to secure our rescue; and the guides evidently believed we were there; yet when the grove was entered they assured the officers that the campfires were two or three days old, and pursuit would be useless. Evidently they did not care to overtake the Indians.

These guides were half-breeds. One of them, familiarly known as Joe Gaboo, had a full-blooded Indian wife. He had a trading-post some twelve miles above Springfield. His wife was seen wearing a shawl, the property of Mrs. Church. From these and other circumstances, it is probable that his sympathies were more with the Indians than with the whites.

Major Williams, in his official report, (see report,) says, the soldiers overtook some straggling squaws, from which it might be inferred that the rest were not far off; also that the trail was strewed with articles of various kinds, taken from the whites; which not only marked the trail, but served to show how recently it had been made. Then, when we remember there was yet considerable snow; and that the Indians not only had horses, but also *travies*, or trailing poles, on which they carried their baggage; it is readily seen that it could not have been difficult to follow the trail, or determine its freshness.

But whether the guides were true or false, or whether or not the soldiers were justifiable in turning back, it was life to us captives. Had they not done so, I should have ended my earthly career then, and this account would never have been written.

No sooner did the Indians discover that an immediate attack was not probable than they began in earnest to prepare for flight. The warriors, taking us with them, proceeded to where the squaws were secreted; called them out, as a partridge would her brood from their hiding-places, gathered up such of the baggage as was deemed most valuable, and struck westward. No time was given us to rest, much less to prepare any food, till some time next day; and we did not camp for two days and nights.

About 3 p. m. of the second day, my strength gave out completely, and when they moved on, after a brief halt to rest, I remained lying on the ground. They beckoned me to follow, but I paid no attention. Then one of the squaws rushed back, furiously brandishing an Indian hoe over my head. The mental and physical sufferings I had already endured had taken away all the fear of death; so I quietly bowed my head, and waited the threatened blow; but seeing the menace did not arouse me she threw down her own pack, seized me by the arm, jerked me to my feet, adjusted the pack, and gave me a tremendous push in the back, sending me forward in the direction the others had gone. She then shouldered her own pack and followed after me.

They, however, went little farther, (perhaps half or three-quarters of a mile,) until they encamped for the night. Some of the *wigwams* were already up when I reached camp.

Thus ended our flight from the United States soldiers, and their attempt to rescue us had only made our situation more terrible.

The following clear and careful statement by Major Flandreau, cannot but interest all lovers of historic truth:

The people at Springfield sent two young men to my agency with the news of the massacre. They brought with them a statement of the facts as related by Mr. Markham, signed by some persons with whom I was acquainted. They came on foot, and arrived at the agency on the 18th of March. The snow was very deep, and was beginning to thaw, which made the travelling extremely difficult. When these young men arrived they were so badly affected with snow-blindness that they could scarcely see at all, and were completely wearied out. I was fully satisfied of the truth of the report that murders had been committed, although the details, of course, were very meagre. I at once held a consultation with Colonel Alexander, commanding the Tenth United States infantry, five or six companies of which were at Fort Ridgley. The colonel, with commendable promptness, ordered Captain Barnard E. Bee with his company to proceed at once to the scene of the massacre, and do all he could either in the way of protecting the settlers or punishing the enemy.

CAPTAIN BEE'S EXPEDITION.

The country between the Minnesota River at Ridgley and Spirit Lake was, at that day, an utter wilderness without an inhabitant. In fact, none of us knew where Spirit Lake was, except that it lay about due south of the fort, at a distance of from 100 to 125 miles.

We procured two guides of experience from among our Sioux half-breeds, Joseph Coursall, more generally known as Joe Gaboo, and Joseph LaFramboise. These men took a pony and a light train to carry the blankets and provisions, put on their snow-shoes, and were ready to go anywhere; while the poor troops with their leather shoes and their back loads, accompanied by a ponderous army-wagon on wheels drawn by six mules, were about as fit for such a march as an elephant is for a ballroom; but it was the best the government had, and they entered upon the arduous duty bravely and cheerfully. I had a light sleigh and a fine team, with my outfit aboard, with a French Canadian voyageur for a driver and old Mr. Prescott for my interpreter, being well outfitted for the occasion, as I always took good care to be while on Indian duty in the winter time. We started on March 19th, at about 1 o'clock, p. m., at first intending to go directly across the country; but we soon decided that course to be utterly impossible as the mules could not draw the wagon through the deep snow. It became apparent that our only hope of reaching the lake was to follow the road down by the way of New Ulm to Mankato, and trust to luck for a road up the Watonwan in the direction of the lake, we having learned that some teams had recently started for that point with supplies. The first days of the march were appalling. The men were wet nearly up to their waists with the deep and melting snow, and utterly weary before they had gone ten miles. Captain Bee was a South Carolinian, and though a veteran had seen most of his service in Mexico and the South. Mr. Murray, his lieutenant, was a gallant young fellow, but had not seen much service.

Neither of them had ever made a snow-camp before; and when we had dug out a place for our first camp, and were making futile efforts to dry our clothes before turning in for the night, I felt that the trip was hopeless. So much time had elapsed since the murders were committed, and so much more would be necessarily consumed before the troops could possibly reach the lake, that I felt assured that no good could result from going on. So I told Captain Bee that if he wanted to return I would furnish him with a written opinion of two of the most experienced voyageurs on the frontier that the march was impossible of accomplishment with the inappropriate outfit with which the troops were furnished. It was then that the stern sense of duty which animates the true soldier exhibited itself in these officers.

The captain agreed with me that the chances of accomplishing any good by going on were very small, but he read his orders, and said, in answer to my suggestion, 'My orders are to go to Spirit Lake and do what I can. It is not for me to interpret my orders, but to obey them. I shall go on until it becomes physically impossible to proceed further. It will then be time to turn back;' and go on he did. We followed the trail up the Watonwan until we found the teams that had made it stuck in a snowdrift, and for the remaining forty or fifty miles the troops marched ahead of the mules, and broke a road for them, relieving the front rank every fifteen or twenty minutes.

When the lake was reached, the Indians were gone. A careful examination was made of their camp and fires by their guides, who pronounced them three or four days old. Their trail led to the west. A pursuit was made by a portion of the command, partly mounted on the mules, and partly on foot; but it was soon abandoned on the declaration of the guides that the Indians were, by the signs, several days in advance. The dead were buried, a guard was established under Lieutenant Murray with 24 men, and Captain Bee with the balance returned to the fort. I learned afterwards from Mrs. Marble, one of the rescued women, that the troops in pursuit came so near that the Indians saw them, and made an ambush for them, and had they not turned back the prisoners would have all been murdered. The guides may have been mistaken in their judgement of the age of the camps and fires, and may have deceived the troops. I knew the young men so well that I have never accused them of a betrayal of their trust; but it was probably best as it was in either case; because had the troops overtaken the Indians the women would have certainly been butchered and some of the soldiers killed. The satisfaction of having killed some of the Indians would not have compensated for this result.

CHAPTER 17

Sad Fate of Mrs. Thatcher

Although the fear of pursuit had subsided, still we journeyed westward, knowing no rest. Frequently breaking the ice with the horses, the Indians waded through, and we followed, where the water was waist-deep. Then, with clothing wet and frozen, we tramped on through wind and storm; lying down at night, in the same clothing, in which we had forded the streams. Often we went without food for two or three days at a time; and when we did get any it was the poorest and most unpalatable. The Indians themselves were never entirely without food long at a time; but we captives got only what they did not care for. No hay was carried, and no grass could yet be found, so the poor horses fared, if possible, worse than we. From time to time, one of them would die of starvation; and then the Indians had meat. But as the horses died our burdens were increased. Such things as they could not put upon the backs of the already overburdened squaws and captives, they buried; marking the place by blazing trees, by boulders, and by streams; etc.

Our journey led through the famous pipe-stone quarry, in Pipestone County, Minnesota. It is situated on a small tributary of the Big Sioux, called Pipestone Creek. The surface of the country is broken and picturesque abounding in bluffs and cliffs. But its principal attraction, of course, is a layer of peculiar and beautiful rock, highly prized by the Indians and no doubt valuable to the whites. The cliffs here are similar to those at Luverne, but smaller. Beneath these, on a level tract of land, is found the precious pipestone. The stratum is about fourteen inches thick, and is overlaid by four feet of other rock, and about two feet of earth, which must be removed before the coveted rock is reached. It is softer than slate, entirely free from grit, and not liable to fracture. When first taken out it is soft, and easily cut with ordinary tools, hardly dulling them more than wood does. On exposure to the air, it becomes hard, and is capable of receiving a high polish. It has already been used for mantels, table-tops, and the like, as well as for ornaments, and is doubtless destined to more extensive use. In colour it varies from light pink to deep, dark red; while some of it is mottled with all these shades, giving great variety.

"The great Red Pipestone Quarry," whence the North American Indians have, from time immemorial, obtained the material for their pipes, has become almost as famous among the white race, being celebrated both in song and story, as among the Indians themselves. This is largely due to the interest which has been excited, among the imaginative and fanciful, by various legends and traditions current among the Indians concerning this locality. Longfellow, in his *Song of Hiawatha*, has rendered some of the strange legends of the Dakotas in unique poetic form, in which read the *Peace Pipe*, in order better to understand the substance of the legend, which I will give for the benefit of my readers.

> *On the mountains of the prairie,*
> *On the great Red Pipestone Quarry,*
> *Gritche Manito, the mighty,*
> *He the Master of Life, descending*
> *On the red crags of the quarry,*
> *Stood erect, and called the nations,*
> *Called the tribes of men together.*
>
> *From the red stone of the quarry*
> *With his hand he broke a fragment,*
> *Moulded it into a pipe head*
> *Shaped and fashioned it with figures.*

Many ages ago the Great Spirit, whose tracks in the form of those of a large bird are yet to be seen upon the rocks, descending from the heavens, stood upon the cliff at the Red Pipestone. A stream issued from beneath his feet, which falling down the cliff passed away in the plain below, while near him, on an elevation, was the Thunder's nest, in which a small bird still sits upon her eggs, the hatching of every one of which causes a clap of thunder. He broke a piece from the ledge and formed it into a huge pipe and smoked it, the smoke rising in a vast cloud so high that it could be seen throughout the earth, and became the signal to all the tribes of men to assemble at the spot from whence it issued, and listen to the words of the Great Spirit. They came in vast numbers and filled the plain below him. He blew the smoke over them all, and told them that the stone was human flesh, the flesh of their ancestors, who were created upon this spot; that the pipe he had made from it was the symbol of peace; that although they should be at war they must ever after meet upon this ground in peace and as friends, for it belonged to them all; they must make their *calumets* from the soft stone and smoke them in their councils, and whenever they wished to appease him or obtain his favour. Having said this he disappeared in the cloud which the last whiff of his pipe had caused, when a great fire rushed over the surface and melted the rocks, and at the same time two squaws passed through the fire to their places beneath the two medicine rocks, where they remain to this day as guardian spirits of the place and must be propitiated by anyone wishing to obtain the pipestone before it can be taken away.

Our captors rested themselves here for about one day, in which time they were engaged in the delightful task of gathering the pipestone and shaping it into pipes, which were formed in the manner foretold ages ago.

The smooth surface of the "Medicine Rocks," are covered with Indian hieroglyphics, of various grotesque forms, representing persons, animals, and turtles, and very many in the form of the tracks of a large bird.

By treaty stipulation, one mile square, including the Red Pipestone quarry, has been ceded to the Yankton Sioux; thus giving them control of this, to them, sacred spot, to which they come from time to time to quarry stone for pipes.

After six weeks of incessant marching over the trackless prairie, and through the deep snow, across creeks, sloughs, rivers, and lakes, we reached the Big Sioux (at about the point where now stands the town of Flandreau). Most of the journey had been performed in cold and inclement weather, but now spring seemed to have come. The vast amount of snow which covered the ground that memorable winter had nearly gone, by reason of the rapid thawing during the last few weeks, causing the river to rise beyond all ordinary bounds, and assume majestic proportions.

The natural scenery along the Big Sioux is grand and beautiful.

From the summit of the bluffs, the eye can view thousands of acres of richest vale and undulating prairie; while through it, winding along like a monstrous serpent, is the river, its banks fringed with maple, oak, and elm. Had we been in a mood to appreciate it, we surely should have enjoyed this beautiful picture. But, alas, how could we! The helpless captives of these inhuman savages could see no beauties in nature, or pleasures in life.

The good Book says, *The tender mercies of the wicked are cruel.* Here we had a sad illustration of the truth of this text.

The trees on the margin of the river are gradually undermined by the constant washing of the water, and bow gracefully over the stream, as if to kiss their shadows. Sometimes these bowing trees, brought down by the wind or their own weight, fall headlong into the stream, and are borne downward by the current. Then, again, the channel is often gorged with ice during the spring freshets, compelling the water to cut for itself a new channel through the soft but heavily timbered bottom-lands. Thus, not merely limbs and logs, but thousands of entire trees, tops, roots, and all, are annually borne off by the Big Sioux. Sometimes these undermined trees cling by their unloosened roots, while their tops reach far into the stream, forming a "boom" across the channel. Against this boom will accumulate a tangled mass of floating timbers, lying in every conceivable position; thus forming a precarious but picturesque bridge; over which one with clear head and steady step may pass with tolerable safety. Yet it is liable to break at any moment, plunging into the turbid stream whomsoever may be upon it; or perhaps to seize, with giant grasp, the hapless victim between the floating timbers.

On such a bridge, we were to cross the now swollen waters. Mrs. Thatcher, whose painful illness and terrible sufferings have been alluded to, had now partially recovered, and was compelled to carry her pack as before. During the six weeks of her captivity, with fortitude heroic and patience surprising, through slush, snow, and ice-cold water; through famine and fatigue, and forced marches; with physical ills that language cannot adequately portray; and with heart-wounds yet deeper, she had been upborne by the hope of yet being restored to her husband and relations. But, alas, for earthly hopes! How often they prove like will-o-the-wisps, that lead on the belated and bewildered traveller, over weary wastes, in vain pursuit; by their very brightness making the darkness more oppressive. All her patient endurance had only brought her here to die a cruel death at last. As we were about to follow the Indians across one of these uncertain bridges, where a single misstep might plunge us into the deep waters, an Indian, not more than sixteen years old, the same who snatched the box of caps from my father, and who had always manifested a great degree of hatred and contempt for the whites, approached us; and taking the pack from Mrs. Thatcher's shoulders, and placing it on his own, ordered us forward.

This seeming kindness at once aroused our suspicions, as no assistance had ever been offered to any of us, under any circumstances whatever. Mrs. Thatcher, being confident that her time had come to die, hastily bade me goodbye, and said: "If you are so fortunate as to escape, tell my dear husband and parents that I desired to live, and escape for their sakes." (It will be remembered that Mr. Thatcher was away from home at the time of the massacre.) When we reached the centre of the swollen stream, as we anticipated, this insolent young savage pushed Mrs. Thatcher from the bridge into the ice-cold water; but by what seemed supernatural strength she breasted the dreadful torrent, and making a last struggle for life reached the shore which had just been left, and was clinging to the root of a tree, at the bank. She was here met by some of the other Indians, who were just coming upon the scene; they commenced throwing clubs at her, and with long poles shoved her back again into the angry stream.

As if nerved by fear, or dread of such a death, she made another desperate effort for life, and doubtless would have gained the opposite shore; but here again she was met by her merciless tormentors, and was beaten off as before. She was then carried down by the furious, boiling current of the Sioux; while the Indians on either side of the stream were running along the banks, whooping and yelling, and throwing sticks and stones at her, until she reached another bridge. Here she was finally shot by one of the Indians in another division of the band, who was crossing with the other two captives, some distance below.

Thus ended the tortures and agonies of poor Mrs. Thatcher, and her sufferings as a captive in the hands of these worse than monsters. Her pure spirit returned to Him who gave it, while her body was borne down the rapid stream, to be devoured by the wild beasts of the plain, or the fishes of the river. In all life's relations and trials she exemplified, most beautifully, all the womanly and Christian graces; and, although she struggled for life, it was not because she feared to meet her God, but rather for the love she bore her husband and kindred. She was only nineteen years of age, just in the morning of life, with

Killing of Mrs. Thatcher in Big Sioux River

all those relations that make life so dear to one; yet she bore all her bereavements, sufferings, and insults with the meekness, patience, and fortitude of the true martyr.

Her cruel murder deeply affected us three remaining captives. We realized, more than ever, how heartless were our captors, and how helpless we were, in their hands; and that at any moment we might meet a like fate. What their motive was, we could not tell. It seemed only an act of wanton barbarity. Stepping, as I was, in her very footsteps at the time, I could not but feel that there was only a step between me and death.

Mrs. Noble was a cousin to Mrs. Thatcher by marriage, and had been intimately associated with her for years. She seemed fairly crushed by this terrible blow, and gave up all hope of deliverance or escape. She became so desperate over our situation that she tried to persuade me to go with her to the river and drown ourselves; but the instruction of a Christian mother came to me, as a heavenly benediction, calming my troubled spirit, restraining me from rashness, and strengthening my faith and hope in the life that is to come.

Benighted and degraded as these savages are, they too believe in the immortality of the soul, and dread the spirits of their victims. An illustration of this occurred in connection with the death of Mrs. Thatcher. One day soon after, some of the squaws took me to dig artichokes near the river. We heard a sound, such as a beaver or otter might make by leaping into the water. As they saw nothing likely to have made the noise, and possibly having some sense of the injustice done to Mrs. Thatcher, they at once concluded it was her spirit, and fled promiscuously, clambering up the high bluff, leaving me and the artichokes behind. When about half way up the hill they halted, and beckoned for me to follow, saying: "*Weahseah wakon minne*," signifying: *Spirit of white woman in the water.* I followed them, but they never went back after the artichokes.

When they reached the camp, they had a wonderful story to tell, about the spirit of the white woman being in the water. And strange to say the *brave Indian warriors* took it at full face value, and no investigation was made into its reliability. Accordingly no more artichokes were dug on the banks of the Big Sioux; and, early the next morning we moved toward the setting sun. Ignorance and superstition, cruelty and cowardly fear, legitimately belong together. Bravery in the true sense of this word, they are ignorant of, as of Egyptian hieroglyphics. They could pelt a defenceless, drowning woman, but would flee in terror from the mere imagination of her disembodied spirit. This, however, plainly teaches us that the belief in the immortality of the soul cannot be entirely obliterated from the human mind (if human these beings can be called).

CHAPTER 18

Rescue of Mrs. Marble

While making this journey, we had frequently met roving parties of Indians, from the various bands of Sioux, who always seemed to be "Hail fellows, well met," with our captors. It has been claimed, by the Sioux generally, that Inkpaduta and his band were "bad Indians," and disfellowshiped by them. But I surely saw nothing of the kind while I was among them. Whenever we met any of the other bands, our captors would go over the story of their achievements, by word, gesture, and the display of scalps and booty, giving a vivid description of the affair; reproducing in fullest detail even the groans and sighs of their victims. To all this the other Sioux listened, not only without any signs of disapprobation, but with every indication of enjoyment and high appreciation.

On the sixth of May, as we were encamped some thirty miles west of the Big Sioux and near a small lake, known to the Indians as *Chaupta-ya-ton-ka*, or Skunk Lake, we were visited by two Sioux brothers, by the name of Ma–kpe-ya-ha-ho-ton and Se-ha-ho-ta, from the reservation on Yellow Medicine River, Minn. They remained overnight, enjoying the hospitality of Inkpaduta; and were especially entertained by a pantomimic representation of the march through, and *heroic* deeds done in, Iowa and Minnesota. After the entertainment was over, the visitors proposed to purchase me, but were informed that I was not for sale. Perhaps they might have bought Mrs. Noble, but in some way got the impression that she was German; and, as is well known, the Sioux have a prejudice against the Teutons. So Mrs. Marble was the favoured one, for whom they paid, as they claimed, all they had—all their trading stock.

Before leaving, she came to the tent where I was, to bid me good-bye, and gave me some account of the negotiations, by which she had changed hands. She told me, also, that she believed her purchasers intended to take her to the whites. She said, if they did, she would do all in her power for our rescue. Though twenty-eight eventful years have passed since that memorable day, the picture of her departure is as vivid in my memory as if it had been yesterday. I see her yet, as she marched away from camp: four Indians in front, and she, in full Indian costume, following in Indian file. But never have I seen her since. Some years ago the report was circulated that she died in an insane asylum. After that it was thought I was the only survivor of the massacre. Although I had made, every effort to learn the truth concerning her, I always failed until January, 1885, when, strange to say, we had the first communication since our captivity. She is now the wife of S. M. Silbaugh, of California, (as at time of first publication). In a letter of recent date, she writes me, describing her capture and rescue, as follows:

Sidell, Napa Co., California,
February 25, 1885.

My Dear Abbie:

Your dear, good letter of January 28th was received in due time, and as you may well suppose it awoke a flood of bitter memories, recalling scenes und events that I have for many years vainly tried to bury in the grave of oblivion. It is nearly twenty-eight years ago since those horrible scenes to which you refer were enacted, and though wrecked in health, and having lost at that time *all* that made life dear to us, we still live, wonderful witnesses of those horrible scenes. With all my horrors, both mental and physical, I have striven through the long years to forget the agonies we endured; but as long as reason remains there are times when these fearful scenes are reproduced in memory with painful fidelity.

It was in the fall of 1856 that I, a young girl lately married, moved with my husband from Linn county to Spirit Lake, on the northern boundary of Iowa, near the line of Minnesota. We located on a piece of land some two or three miles from any other settlers. Here we fondly hoped to make a home, induce other settlers to come, and hew the way for civilization. Alas! how little we know what is in store for us. The following winter was one of uncommon severity, the snow was very deep, and weather intensely cold. Cattle perished with cold and hunger;

lakes and rivers froze over; and the scattering settlers remained in their log-cabins, fearing to attempt the dreadful elements, even for a brief ride of a few miles.

In the month of March the Indian outbreak occurred. It is with feelings unutterable that I recall to memory the morning of the thirteenth day of March, 1857. On that sad day I lost all that lent to life a charm—home, husband, health, love, peace of mind, and everything, save existence itself. This alone with reason was spared to me, and why? I have often asked myself the question. God in His infinite wisdom alone knows.

For your sake, dear Abbie, I will once again tear aside the vail that has shrouded those scenes, and go over again, as well as memory will permit, a recital of the horrible atrocities enacted, and the agonies I endured.

It was just after breakfast, and my husband and I had partaken of our cheerful meal in our sunny little cabin. Little did we dream of danger, or that the stealthy and murderous savages were then nearing our happy home. But, being attracted by noise outside, we looked through the window and saw, with fearful forebodings, a band of painted warriors nearing the door. Knowing nothing of the massacre, though the outbreak had commenced five days before, my husband stepped to the door, spoke to the leader of the band, and welcomed them to the house. A number came, and one of them perceived my husband's rifle, a handsome one. The Indian immediately offered to trade; the trade was made on his own terms. My husband gave him $2.50 extra.

The Indian then proposed to shoot at a mark, and signalled to my husband to put up the target. It was then that the fearful work began, for while putting up the target the fiendish savage levelled his gun and shot my noble husband through the heart. With a scream, I rushed for the door to go to him, but two brawny savages barred my passage and held fast the door. But love and agony were stronger than brute force, and with frantic energy I burst the door open, and was soon kneeling by the side of him who a few minutes before was my loving and beloved husband. But before I reached him a merciful God had released his spirit from mortal agony. He wore a belt around his waist containing a thousand dollars in gold. This belt was soaked with his precious blood.

The Indians immediately took possession of the money, and entering the house they began searching for valuables. They took what they desired. They first found my gold watch, and taking it apart they used the wheels for ornaments. They took quilts, blankets, provisions, and everything that pleased their savage fancy. They gave me to understand that for the present they would not kill me, but I must accompany them.

Having committed their diabolical deeds and plundered my house, they placed me, broken-hearted and crushed, on a pony in their midst, and the march commenced. I cannot attempt to describe the feelings with which I looked for the last time on the mutilated body of my husband as it was left, crushed and beaten into the snow, by fiends who disgrace the name of human beings.

As we left the spot which had so lately been associated to me by the sacred name of home, the brutal savages fastened my red stand-cover to a pole as a flag or trophy, and picked up my husband's cap that had so lately covered his beautiful raven locks. They kicked it before them for perhaps a mile. It seemed to be done in mockery of my intense sufferings.

I now come to the part of this terrible history, dear Abbie, where I met you—a sweet innocent girl of fourteen years,—Mrs. Thatcher, and Mrs. Noble. We met, oh loving friend, as pitiful captives in an Indian camp!

Perhaps you remember that while we were camped at a little lake the Indians went to Springfield and massacred the people and robbed that place. I do not know the name of the lake, but I remember it was surrounded with large oak trees, in which there were a number of eagles' nests. I do not know whether you recollect their arrival in camp that evening or not, but I remember it well, and as long us reason retains her throne I shall never forget it. It was just about sundown, and I had stepped out of the tent, when through the opening of the oaks my eyes caught the sight of a long line of dusky objects coming across the prairie.

A second glance, and I recognized the Indians of our camp. They came single file to the number of some twelve or thirteen. Each one led a horse, which with their drag-poles, on which they carry their loads, made a long line of men and horses. The horses were loaded with all kinds of goods and plunder.

It was evident a dry-goods store had been robbed. For, if you remember, each Indian wore a full suit of new dark clothes, and with the new dark cape drawn closely down over their brows they presented a singular and really gloomy appearance. Many of them even wore new gloves. They brought blankets, groceries of all kinds, and whole bolts of prints. I with my own hands made up dozens of garments of the calico: dresses for their *papooses*, and shirts for the men, as well as dresses for the squaws. They had also, many of them, a young animal strapped to their horses. I soon perceived that they were young calves. You doubtless remember they feasted about this time on veal cooked with the hair and hide on.

Now, in regard to the death of Mrs. Thatcher, I did not see her until she was in the water. I was some distance below. On reaching the river I noticed an Indian shooting at an object in the water. I attracted his attention, and pointing to the object, remarked in Indian, '*Budot*' (meaning otter), when he answered, '*Hea hea, Wasecha*' white woman. I then saw, to my horror and dismay, that it was one of the white captives, and soon recognized by her dress that it was Mrs. Thatcher. He was still shooting at her, but I think that she was already dead.

I will now give you a brief description of my rescue. One afternoon as I stepped out of the tent I saw two fine-looking, well-dressed Indians. I spoke to them, and soon perceived they had taken a fancy to me, and desired to buy me. The trade was made in guns, blankets, powder, etc., quickly done, and I was made to understand that I was the property of the two strange Indians. I found we were to start immediately, and then, if you remember, I stepped to you and told you I was bought by them, and if I ever reached civilization that I would do all in my power to effect your rescue and that of Lydia; a promise I fulfilled as soon as possible, but, to my great horror, the relief party came too late to benefit poor Lydia.

On leaving the camp of Inkpaduta, two of his Indians accompanied the friendly Indians and myself for the solo purpose, it proved, to secure the remainder of the purchase price. It was evident the friendly Indians feared the savages would regret their trade, and for this reason I was pushed on as rapidly as possible. It was about 3 p. m. when we started. Sometime after dark a halt was made and we partook of a frugal repast of parched corn provided by the friendly Indians. We then lay down for a short sleep, myself perched between the two friendly Indians. It was evident they feared treachery.

Before daybreak the march was ordered, and we arose and without a bite for refreshment a rapid march commenced. About 9 o'clock a. m. we arrived on the bank of the Big Sioux River. On the opposite bank was an encampment of Indians. I may here state, this whole journey, a long sixty miles, we travelled from the savage camp, was made over burned prairie, and as my *moccasins* were worn to shreds my bleeding feet were pierced through with the sharp stubbles.

We crossed the river in a canoe, the savages going with one of the friendly Indians first. The canoe returned, and the other one and myself went over. As we started across my rescuer threw back my blanket from my shoulders, to make all the display possible, so as the Indians could all see they had purchased and rescued a white woman. It was evident they were very proud of their new possession. I soon found that fortune had vastly changed for me. All honours and courtesies known to them were showered upon me. A bountiful repast of corn, cooked and served in wooden bowls, with horn spoons, was set before us. It seemed approaching a shade of civilization. I thought food had never tasted so good before.

Soon after this a Frenchman came to the door of the tent, and in good English said, 'Come to my house now.' I went, but found only a tent, yet to my great pleasure his neat little squaw served me a cup of hot tea, some potatoes, and dried pumpkins, cooked. Surely, I thought this is a feast fit for the gods! A great contrast from my former experience with Inkpaduta, where we subsisted mostly on digging roots, and roasting bones and feathers, to keep soul and body together.

After the repast, and the departure of Inkpaduta's Indians, it was thought best to move camp for fear they might attack us, and endeavour to regain their captive. On the journey we came to another Indian camp. Here new honours were heaped upon me. A fine new blanket was presented me. A dog-feast was ordered in a tent in the midst of hosts of Sioux warriors. I, the only woman, received the toast and listened to the speeches and partook of the feast, which was tendered to me by the hands of the chief. The only recompense asked was, the chief desired me to mention him favourably to the Great Father at Washington, should I go there. We then took up our line of march again, and after several days reached the Yellow Medicine.

Here were the parents of the two Indians who had rescued me, and they gave me into their charge. They had shortly before lost a daughter, and it seems their intentions were to adopt me in her place. Every kindness possible was shown me. I soon found myself in the position of an Indian princess. A snug apartment was fitted out for my use. A couch of fine robes was prepared, and real pillows of softest feathers. The room was curtained off from the main tent by print curtains. My food was cooked, and the bones even taken from the meat before passed into my apartment. I remained here about two weeks, and was made to know by their actions it was their desire to keep me as their daughter.

At this place was a government store, and one day an Indian, clerk, I think, of the store, visited me to go to the store to present me a dress-pattern. It appears, during my stay here, word had been sent that a white woman rescued from the Indians was in the camp at Yellow Medicine. Between two and three weeks after my rescue, Messrs. Riggs and Williamson, missionaries of the agency, at Hazelwood, came to see me, and, buying me a suit of clothing, soap, and other articles, took me to visit in their families. I was formally passed over to the whites by my Indian father, who accompanied me, and in the presence of a number of white people kissed me, and shedding tears bade me farewell.

I was then virtually free and among my own people.

I learned that the sum of $1,000 had been paid by the state of Minnesota for me. I soon after accompanied Major Flandreau to St. Paul, where every evidence of sympathy and kindness was showered upon me by everyone I met.

Believe me ever your own true friend,

M. A. Silbaugh.

It was perhaps three weeks after our capture, when our own clothing actually became worn out, and we were compelled to adopt the costume of the squaws, a style of dress having, at least, one thing in its favour: it was better adapted to our mode of life than that of the civilized nations. Trailing skirts may be the proper thing in the drawing-room, carpeted with brussels, but in the *drawing-room* of the Sioux, or on one of their tours, just between winter and spring time, they would hardly be found either healthful or convenient. Experience has probably taught them the advantage of their costume. This costume I will describe.

The dress of the males, ordinarily, consists of deer-skin leggings, having the resemblance of the lower half of a pair of pantaloons; *moccasins* cover the feet, and complete the dress of the lower extremities. A belt or girdle surrounds the waist, and under this is drawn a piece of blue broad-cloth, about a quarter of a yard in width, and a yard and a half in length, or long enough to pass between the lower extremities, and the ends fall over, and form a flap in front, and on the back of the lower portion of the body. A short skirt of buckskin—sometimes fringed around the bottom—and a blanket, complete the outfit of the men. In addition to this, however, may be seen a fathom of scarlet or blue cloth, worn around the waist, as a sash; and another of like material, or a shawl, around the head, as a turban.

With the female a calico chemise covers the arms and body a little below the waist; a skirt of blue broad-cloth is confined around the waist by a belt or girdle, and extends nearly to the ankles: a pair of red or blue pantalets and *moccasins* complete the under-dress. To this is added a blanket, or fathom of red and blue broadcloth to be used as an outer garment or wrap. With this the usual dress of the squaw is complete. Their blankets are white, red, blue, or green; composed of fine wool, and of superior fabrication.

Our shoes were taken from us immediately after our capture, and *moccasins* given us instead, so that we should not make "shoe-tracks," as before stated. A *moccasin* will wear through in a couple of days, and need mending. They would sit up at night, after a long day's march, and dry and mend their *moccasins*. But night always found me too exhausted for that; and as soon as we were settled for the night I would fall asleep. Next day as I would go limping, with bleeding feet, they would tell me that if I had mended my *moccasins*, as they did, I need not now go lame.

I missed Mrs. Marble's presence very much, but did not grieve, as formerly, for poor Mrs. Thatcher, nor as subsequently for Mrs. Noble; for I trusted she had, at least, bettered her condition by the change, if she had not really gained her liberty. Of one thing I was certain, she could not fall into worse hands than those from which she had escaped.

She was at once taken, by her purchasers, to the agency on the Yellow Medicine, and delivered into the hands of Stephen R. Riggs and Dr. Williamson, missionaries stationed at that place. Here, the various tribes of the Sioux were accustomed to assemble to receive their annuities, and all the business between them and the United States was transacted. These missionaries immediately delivered Mrs. Marble into the hands of Charles E. Flandreau, United States Indian agent for the Sioux.

There was an understanding with her purchasers that they should be amply rewarded. This agreement was carried out; the two Indians receiving five hundred dollars each. At the agency she laid aside the habiliments of savagery and serfdom, donning the attire of freedom and civilization.

The major took her in his buggy to St. Paul, where he generously ordered for her a rich and more becoming habiliment of widowhood, in which to appear before the public. Excitement ran high. Hundreds crowded the hotel where she stopped, to offer their congratulations, and express their sympathies.

The legislature then in session appropriated, from an empty treasury, ten thousand dollars, to be used (all or part, as occasion might require,) for the rescue of the two remaining captives, and to compensate for the one already brought in.

Many other important and interesting facts concerning her rescue from the Indians are given by Hon. C. E. Flandreau, and her purchasers, as follows:

Mrs. Marble Brought In.

I was engaged in devising plans for the rescue of the captives and the punishment of the Indians, in connection with Colonel Alexander, of the 10th Infantry, but had found it very difficult to settle upon any course which would not endanger the safety of the prisoners. We knew that any hostile demonstration would be sure to result in the destruction of the women, and were without means to fit out an expedition for their ransom. While we were deliberating upon the best course to pursue, an accident opened the way to success. A party of my Indians were hunting on the Big Sioux River, and having learned that Inkpaduta's band were encamped at Lake Chau-pta-ya-ton-ka, about thirty miles west of the river, and also knowing of the fact that they held some white women prisoners, two young men (brothers) visited the camp, and after much talk they succeeded in purchasing Mrs. Marble. They paid for her all they possessed, and brought her into the agency, and delivered her into the possession of the missionaries stationed at that point. She was at once turned over to me with a written statement from the two Indians who had brought her in, which was prepared for them at their request by Mr. Riggs, who spoke their language fluently. I will allow them to tell their own story. It was as follows:

Hon. C. E. Flandreau:

Father: In our spring hunt, when encamped at the north end of Big Wood on the Sioux River, we learned from some Indians who came to us that we were not far from Red End's camp. Of our own accord, and contrary to the advice of all about us, we concluded to visit them, thinking that possibly we might be able to obtain one or more of the white women held by them as prisoners. We found them encamped at Chan-pta-ya-ton-ka Lake, about thirty miles west of our own camp. We were met at some distance from their lodges by four men armed with revolvers, who demanded of us our business. After satisfying them that we were not spies, and had no evil intentions in regard to them, we were taken into Ink-paduta's lodge.

The night was spent in reciting their massacre, etc. It was not until the next morning that we ventured to ask for one of the women. Much time was spent in talking, and it was not until the middle of the afternoon did we obtain their consent to our proposition. We paid for her all we had.

We brought her to our mother's tent, clothed her as we were able, and fed her bountifully with the best we had, duck and corn. We brought her to Lac qui Parle, and now, father, after having her with us fifteen days, we place her in your hands.

It was perilous business for which we think we should be liberally rewarded. We claim for our services $500 each. We do not want it in horses. They would be killed by jealous warriors. We do not want it in ammunition and goods; these we should be obliged to divide with others.

The labourer is worthy of his own reward. We want it in money, which we can make more serviceable to ourselves than it could be in any other form. This is what we want to say.

Ma-Kpe-Ya-Ha-Ho-Ton.

Se-Ha-Ho-Ta.

In the above statement and demand, we the undersigned—father of the young men, and father-in-law to one of them—concur.

Wa-Kan-Va-Ne, **X** his mark.

Non-Pa-Kin-Yan, **X** his mark.

May 21, 1857.'

EFFORTS TO RESCUE THE OTHER CAPTIVES.

By the action of these Indians we not only got one of the captives, but we learned for the first time definitely the whereabouts of the marauders and the assurance that the other women were still alive, as these Indians had seen them in Red End's camp.

The legislature of the territory was in session, and the interest in the fate of the captured women was very active at the capital. Of course there was no end of people who knew just how to rescue them, and also exactly how to annihilate the Indians. There always are such people on such occasions. Public sentiment received its expression through the legislature, which on the 15th day of May passed an act appropriating $10,000, or so much thereof as was necessary, out of an empty treasury, to be applied to the rescue of the captives. Fortunately the appropriation was not hampered by any condition, or adoption of any of the numerous plans suggested to assume it, but the governor was given *carte blanche* to do what he thought best with it.

NOVEL FINANCIERING.

At the time I received Mrs. Marble, on the 21st of May, from her deliverers, I had not heard of this appropriation; but the way seemed open to rescue the remaining captives. I at once called for volunteers from among my Indians to go out and buy them, which I knew was the only way they could be obtained alive. The first difficulty I had to overcome was to satisfy the demand of the two brothers for Mrs. Marble, as I wanted to use them in my proposed expedition. I had no public fund that could be devoted to such a purpose; but I had confidence in the generosity of the people, especially if I succeeded. As every moment might be worth a life, I determined to assume the responsibility of anything that was necessary. I was ably assisted by Messrs. Biggs and Williamson, both in excellent advice, and in the exertion of their influence with the Indians.

The traders all responded cheerfully to my call upon them. I could not raise $1000 in money in the country, but I had $500; and, in order to raise the other $500 to pay the two. Indians for Mrs. Marble, we resorted to a novel mode of financiering. Mr. Riggs and myself decided to issue a territorial bond for the amount, drawn on hope and charity, payable in three months from date. It was the first bond ever issued by the territory, and I am happy to say, although executed without authority, it met with a better fate than some which have followed it under the broad seal of the state: it was paid at maturity. As it was the first obligation of the territory, and being rather original in form I give it in full:

> I, Stephen R. Riggs, missionary of the Sioux Indians, and I, Charles E. Flandreau, U. S. Indian agent for the Sioux, being satisfied that Makpeyahahoton and Sehahota, two Sioux Indians, have performed a valuable service to the territory of Minnesota, and humanity, by rescuing from captivity Margaret Ann Marble and delivering her to the Sioux agent; and being further satisfied that the rescue of the two remaining white women who are now in captivity among Inkpaduta's band of Indians, depends much upon the liberality of the Territory of Minnesota, through its government and citizens, have this day paid to said above named Indians the sum of $500 in money, and do hereby pledge to said two Indians, that the further sum of $500 will be paid to them by the Territory of Minnesota, or its citizens, within three months from date hereof.
>
>
>
> Dated May 22nd, 1857, at Pajutajiji, M. T.
>
> Stephen R. Riggs, A. B. F. M.
>
> Chas. E. Flandreau,
>
> U. S. Agent for Sioux.
>
>

The cash and this paper paid for Mrs. Marble, and the magnificence of the ransom, produced the effect I had anticipated. Volunteers were not wanting. I selected Mazintemani, who was one of the pillars of Mr. Biggs' church; John Other Day, (who was such a friend of the whites at the time of the Minnesota massacre of 1862, as to be rewarded by the state with a quarter section of land,) and Hotonwashta.

The question of outfit then presented itself, and I ran my credit with the traders for the following articles at the prices stated.

Wagon	$ 110 00
Four horses	600 00
Twelve 3 point blankets, 4 blue and 8 white	56 00
Thirty-two yds of squaw cloth	44 00
Thirty-seven and a half yds of calico	5 37
Twenty pounds of tobacco	10 00
One sack of shot	4 00
One dozen shirts	13 00
Ribbon	4 00
Fifteen pounds of powder	25 00
Corn	4 00
Flour	10 00
Coffee	1 50
Sugar	1 50

With this outfit, and instructions to give as much of it as was necessary for the women, my expedition started on the 23rd day of May, from Yellow Medicine.

I at once left for Fort Ridgley, to consult Colonel Alexander, as to the plan of operation for an attack upon the camp of Inkpaduta, the instant we could get word as to the safety of the white women. The colonel entered into the spirit of the matter with zeal. He had four or five companies at the fort, and proposed to put them into the field so as to approach Skunk Lake, where Inkpaduta had his camp, from several different directions, and insure his destruction.

If an event which was wholly unforeseen had not transpired, the well laid plan of Colonel Alexander would undoubtedly have succeeded. But, unfortunately for the cause of justice, just about the time we began to expect information from my expedition, which was the signal for moving on the enemy, an order arrived at the fort, commanding the colonel, with all his available force, to start immediately and join the expedition against the Mormons, which was then moving to Utah, under the command of General Sidney Johnston. So peremptory was the command that the steamboat which brought the order carried off the entire garrison of the fort, and put an end to all hopes of our being able to punish the enemy.

CHAPTER 19

Superstitions and Manners of the Dakotas

After the departure from Inkpaduta's camp of the two Yellow Medicine Indians and Mrs. Marble, we proceeded on our journey. We were now far beyond the Big Sioux, in Dakota territory, and probably beyond where any white man had ever been. The provisions taken from the whites had long been exhausted, and our only subsistence was furnished by such edible roots as had survived the winter, and whatever animals or wild fowl we could find on the way. We passed through an Indian village on one occasion, in Minnesota, where the squaws had planted and raised a small patch of corn. Here, about half a teacup full was boiled and given to me, the first morsel I had eaten in three days.

The principal root we had was wild artichoke. They also got two or three other kinds of roots, one, although growing in the ground, resembled beans; another being longer and more irregular in form, and of a light colour, nearly white. All these were roasted, boiled, or eaten raw, as fancy or convenience led them to do. Unpalatable as these roots were, but for them we must have famished.

Among the game killed and greedily devoured were geese, ducks, swans, brants, pelicans, and cranes, of the fowl kind; and of quadrupeds there were beaver, otter, musk-rat, skunk, etc., and fish. The fowls were prepared for the kettle by simply pulling off the roughest of the feathers, without washing or dressing. They were eaten without salt or seasoning. Beaver and otter were singed to free them of the thickest of the fur, pitched into a pot, and boiled.

When cooked these savoury meats were dished out into wooden bowls, each bowl holding a quart or more, and eaten with spoons made of buffalo horns.

Each Indian has his place in the *wigwam*, into which he drops as regularly as cattle into their stalls in a stable. The squaws dish up the food into these bowls, and hand them to their lordly masters, who sit and eat the meat, and drink the soup, and pass up their dishes for more until the supply is gone.

Most savoury among these savoury meats was the polecat or skunk. I well remember, on one occasion, going on a skunk-hunt. It was a warm evening, when they would be likely to be out of their holes. Just a little before sundown one of the squaws came to me, told me she was going after skunks, and ordered me to accompany her. She was armed with a club, but I went unarmed, to carry the game. The dusky huntress was not long in scenting her game, and she took after it like a bloodhound. It struck for cover; she after it. Just as it entered its hole she struck, but missed her prey, and broke her club. It was full a quarter of a mile to timber where a new club could be obtained. So she left me to prevent the escape of the game while she went for arms. Her instructions were explicit and peremptory: if he came to the mouth of the hole I was to strike at him and drive him back. I lay down by the hole to watch, of course, but only too glad of a chance to rest, and most sincerely hoping he would escape.

She had been gone but a little while when the aromatic little fellow poked his nose out of the hole. I kept as still as a mouse. After concluding that the coast was clear he trotted off, so saving his own dear life, and saving me from the necessity of helping to eat him. In due time the chief of this little hunting party returned, fully prepared to cope with the game she had driven to cover, and inquired of me if he was still there. Thinking *honesty the best policy,* I shook my head, and pointed off in the way he had gone. To say she was angry is to put it mildly. She fairly danced with rage, showered upon me a perfect torrent of invectives, and gesticulated in a manner indescribable. It is a wonder she did not use on me the club she had been to so much pains to get, but for unaccountable reasons I escaped the blows, and was heartily glad Mr. Skunk was gone. Had she known that I purposely allowed him to escape I would, doubtless, have felt the full weight of her club. By this time it was too dark for further operations, so we went back to camp without the coveted luxury; and I was never taken on a skunk-hunt again.

We were absolutely compelled to eat whatever was given to us, or to dispose of it unknown to them. Frequently they would give me things I could not possibly swallow, for instance, fish, of which the flesh was so decomposed it was falling from the bone. In such cases I would watch my opportunity and drop it inside my blanket, from which I would throw it away when on the march. Possibly skunk-meat might not be so bad, if properly dressed; but singed and boiled entire, it was almost too savoury to suit my taste.

When the Indians came to my father's house, they brought with them a sick *papoose*, about eight or nine years old. How long it had then been sick I do not know, but from its emaciation and weakness, I should judge, some time. They then had two sleds, in one of which this *papoose* was carried. As the snow melted away, they left the sleds, substituting "*travies*." As this term may be new to the reader I will give a brief explanation.

The long poles used in the construction of their *teepes* are made into small bundles by being bound together at the ends. Then two of these bundles are attached to a strong thong of rawhide long enough to go around a horse's neck where the collar usually goes. The poles are so attached as to be a foot or more apart, and when the thong is fastened at the horse's neck, the smaller ends of the poles will be at his shoulders, while the others will drag on the ground. The *travies*, a large hoop, oval in shape, and woven across with bark or buckskin, are attached to the poles, just back of the horse's heels. On this were placed such articles as they did not choose to carry, or such persons as were not able to walk.

The loads which even ponies were made to haul in this awkward manner were immense. Besides these heavy loads on the *travies*, it is not unusual to see an Indian on the back of the pony, and heavy laden baskets at the sides. Even the dogs were made to haul smaller *travies*, yet large enough to be perfectly barbarous. The poor creatures would pull, as if for dear life, until perfectly exhausted, when they would drop to the ground, as if dead, and lie there a few minutes, then get up and trudge on again. Thus, day after day, these half-fed animals were made to toil to the utmost limit of possible endurance for their lazy masters.

But to return to the sick *papoose*. In regard to the death of Mrs. Thatcher, we saw some of their superstition. In the case of this *papoose* we see yet others. They would gather cedar twigs and burn them in the *teepe*, near the couch of the sick one, as a method of divination. The omen seemed to be good or ill, according as the smoke went, from or toward the sick. The first time that I remember of their trying this, the smoke accidentally drew toward the fire, and so away from the couch, which I soon saw pleased them; they pointed to the smoke, motioned in the direction it went, and by their lively gibberish, and expressive faces, showed that they were perfectly delighted.

As, however, the *papoose* did not recover, some days later they got the medicine-man again, and repeated the experiment, but with less satisfactory results. This time, for some reason, the smoke was borne toward the *papoose*, whereupon every Indian in the tent commenced howling, as only an Indian can. This was to them, evidently, a bad omen—a sign that the child would die. It died; so to them the sign proved true.

On one occasion, as the *papoose* was unwrapped, at the close of the day's march, they evidently thought it was dead, as the mother broke out in the song of death, and the father seized his gun and started off in great rage, as we supposed, to kill himself; as the other Indians ran after him, seized his gun, and brought him back. The *papoose* was found, however, to be still alive (though chilled and nearly dead). So the parents were quieted for the time. Perhaps it was a week or ten days after this, that the *papoose* actually died; and then the mother cut off her coarse black hair, as a sign of mourning, and the death-wail broke out in earnest. Their death-song is a wild, hideous succession of cadences, utterly unlike the plaints of despair or grief, but rather a wild, unearthly sound, expressive of only savage passion, impressive to witness and startling to hear. Every night at the same hour, for several weeks, this passionate wailing was repeated. The mother would begin; then others, one after another, would break out in the wild wail, until not only those in the *teepe*, where the death occurred, but also those in other *teepes*, who were related to the deceased, had joined in the lamentations. Thus, for weeks, the twilight hours were made hideous by these horrible sounds, which, once heard, can never be forgotten.

After death, the body was still borne on the *travies* for several days, closely wrapped in a blanket. When we reached the desired grove, a platform was constructed of poles laid across two horizontal limbs of a large oak tree, and, by means of strips of bark tied to the body, it was hauled up for burial. There the poor emaciated body was laid to rest, after having been dragged around so long. And thus the Sioux bury their dead.

Speaking of this *papoose* suggests the treatment of *papooses* in general. A Sioux mother binds her infant to a small board when a few hours old. It is first imbedded in the feathery heads of the cat-tail flag (picked to pieces), and wrapped around with strips of cloth or buckskin, commencing at the feet, and extending upward until all but the head is enveloped. It is then placed on a board, and firmly bound with a blanket. This keeps it straight, protects it from injury in the rough treatment it receives, and is altogether more convenient for their mode of living than any other arrangement. From this confined position they are relieved only for a few minutes at a time, and this only at long intervals.

When old enough to run alone, it is relieved of its swathing bands, and if the weather is warm it is turned loose, without an article of clothing to protect or impede the action of its limbs. In the *teepes* the *papooses* are stood up against the wall, even from the first, and are almost no trouble at all. On the march they are stuck in the panniers on the horses; or on the backs of the squaws, inside of their blankets, or in any manner convenience may suggest.

When I came to see how the children were *educated*, and what was the early *home-training* (if home they can be said to have) I ceased to wonder at their savagery. From their earliest childhood they are taught that fighting and killing are the highest virtues. The war-dance is a school eminently adapted to this end. There, all the fierce and cruel deeds in which each has participated are recited in a manner that might

> *Stir a fever in the blood of age,*
> *Or make an infant's sinews strong as steel.*

Not only this, but the private recitals, around the fire in the *teepes*, and all the intercourse of the children with each other, their sports, (if sports they can be called,) tend to the same end.

Occasionally there would be a day so cold and stormy that even a Sioux would not travel. These were to me more dreaded, even, than the wearisome marches, because of being crowded in the *teepe*, by the side of the young scions, with their dirty faces and noses; who here had a good opportunity of developing their true nature. There were "wars and rumours of wars" from morning till night. They would fight, pull hair, scratch, and bite until their faces were smeared with blood; the squaws not only making no attempt to restrain them, but actually cheering and urging them on; laughing in great glee when they got in some lucky hit, or if they showed fierce or revengeful dispositions. With such training, is it strange that they grow to be what they are? *As the twig is bent, the tree is inclined.*

The highest ambition of the young warrior is to secure the "feather," which is the testimonial of his having murdered some human being; but securing one feather only whets his zeal for more, as his rank or standing depends upon the number of his feathers. These are worn in the hair until enough are obtained to make a cap, or headgear. No one would be allowed to wear a feather which did not represent a life taken, any more than in our regular army a captain would be allowed to wear the shoulder-straps of a colonel. The head-dress, filled with these eagle-feathers and other insignia of blood, is regarded as "*Wakan*," (most sacred,) and no unhallowed hand of man or woman dare touch it.

It seems to me that Christian statesmen, and all those who have a duty to perform toward the rising generation in civilized nations, might find a lesson in this. Is there not altogether too much glorification of deeds of blood? Too much talk about gunpowder and glory? Patriotism is a noble emotion; but love of country is one thing; love of war is quite another.

The religious beliefs of the Dakotas is a profound study; worthy of an older head than mine was; yet there was much that could not but interest and impress me. The following statement of these beliefs is given, not simply on my own authority as the result of my own observation while among them, but on the authority of Philander Prescott, U. S. government interpreter of the expedition sent from Fort Ridgley, for the relief of Springfield.

For forty-five years this man was intimately associated with them; married one of their number; and spoke their language better than they did themselves. He was thus familiar with all their beliefs and customs, and his statements are most reliable. In the massacre of 1862, at the age of nearly seventy, he was murdered in cold blood by those he had so faithfully served for nearly half a century. He talked with his fiendish murderers, and tried to reason with them by saying:

> I am an old man; I have lived among you forty-five years; I have never done you any harm, but have ever been your true friend in all your troubles. My wife and children are of your own blood. Why do you want to kill me?

But the iron heart of the savage knows no pity, no mercy; and while he was thus remonstrating with them he received the fatal bullet, and died a martyr at the hands of that perfidious race, with no other reason given him, for taking his life, than that he was a white man, and "the white man must die."

The Sioux believe in one Great Spirit, the maker of heaven and earth. They also believe in subordinate spirits, both good and bad, and in the immortality of the soul. The Great Spirit, they believe, created everything except wild rice and thunder. The rice, they believe to be beneath the workmanship of the Great One, and attribute it to chance. Thunder they believe to be the sound of the wings of an immense bird.

They believe that somewhere in the heavens are cities and villages, where the spirits of the departed remain at war with their enemies; and where the Sioux will always find plenty of game. They believe the spirits of the dead have power to inflict injury. They therefore offer sacrifices, to appease them.

They adore the Great Spirit, although they have distorted conceptions of the attributes of the Deity. Various objects, animate and inanimate, are worshiped. Sometimes they think the Great Spirit angry with them, as when storms do them harm. They then make sacrifices of animals and other things to pacify him, that they may prosper in life.

They support a non-hereditary sacerdotal order; the same person being both priest and medicine-man. They have also what may be termed jugglers, who, they believe, have power to confer blessings or curses. They have little conception of rewards and punishments after death.

In cases of sickness, they perform ceremonies, which are expected to cure the sick. They also believe in dreams and omens. When they have a good dream, they suppose some friendly spirit has been near them; but bad dreams indicate that of an enemy. The bat they regard as an evil omen, and dread the *ignis fatuus*, believing it a certain sign of death in the family of the one who sees it.

In war, or hunting, they are directed by signs and dreams. These signs may be, the running of animals, flying of birds, or sounds at night. They think some animals have souls, and that the bear has four; but do not believe in the transmigration of souls as do some of the people of Asia.

Their fabled monsters are: Haokuk, the giant, and Unkatahe. The giant could stand astride the tallest pine-tree, or the broadest river; lives on the fat of animals; and is armed with a huge bow and arrow. They believe he yet lives, and can kill them with a look from his piercing eye. The Unkatahe is an animal of two kinds, one of the water

125

and one of the land. They are supposed to possess great power, and can even kill the thunder. They also believe in fairies who inhabit all strange places, in rivers, lakes, cliffs, mountains, and forests.

The manners, customs, and institutions of the Dakotas have many of the patriarchal features of the ancients. They strictly observe the feast of first fruits; and all animals offered in sacrifice must be the best. In some of the feasts they are obliged to eat all that has been cooked. After a religious feast incense is offered; the host taking a large coal from the fire, upon which the foliage of the cedar is laid, and with this the vessels are perfumed. Certain animals they regard with great veneration: among these, the serpent, turtle, wolf, grizzly bear, and eagle.

In customs, language, traditions, and physiognomy, the Sioux differ radically from the Algonquins. So marked is this difference that Pike, Schoolcraft, and others have expressed the opinion that they are a distinct race. Their sacrifices and supplications to the unknown God, their feasts, burnt offerings, incense, and certain customs of the females, remind one of the customs and observances among the Asiatic tribes before the Christian era. Pike expressed the opinion that they are of Tartarian origin. They are the Arabs of the western plains.

CHAPTER 20

Death of Mrs. Noble

As before stated, we from time to time met with strange bands of Sioux, of the various subordinate tribes. Hence, in about four weeks after the departure of Mrs. Marble, we fell in with a small party of Yanktons. One of them by the name of Wanduskaihanke, or End-of-the-snake, purchased Mrs. Noble and myself. What he paid I never knew. His motive was to make money by selling us to the whites. Unfortunately our purchaser did not take an immediate departure, as did the purchaser of Mrs. Marble, but continued to journey with Inkpaduta. Now, for the first time since our captivity, Mrs. Noble and I were allowed to lodge in the same *teepe*. Our owner treated us about the same as our former masters, and we were required to trudge along and carry a pack as before. Our master was a one-legged Indian, and having no artificial limb he hobbled about on a crutch.

It might be well said, he lived on his horse. He went hunting mounted, and his squaw, or one of us captives, had to follow after and pick up the game. I have followed after him many a weary mile for this purpose. If any game was shot in the water, his dog, being trained for that purpose, would bring it out to the shore, where I would take it and carry it on. One evening, a few days after we were sold, just as we supposed we were settled for the night, and as Mrs. Noble and I were about to lie down to rest, a son of Inkpaduta, of the name of Makpea-hotoman, or Roaring Cloud, came into the tent of the Yankton, and ordered Mrs. Noble out. She shook her head and refused to go. I told her she had better, as I feared he would kill her if she did not. But she still refused.

Mrs. Noble was the only one of us whoever dared to refuse obedience to our masters. Naturally of an independent nature, and conscious of her superiority to her masters in everything except brute

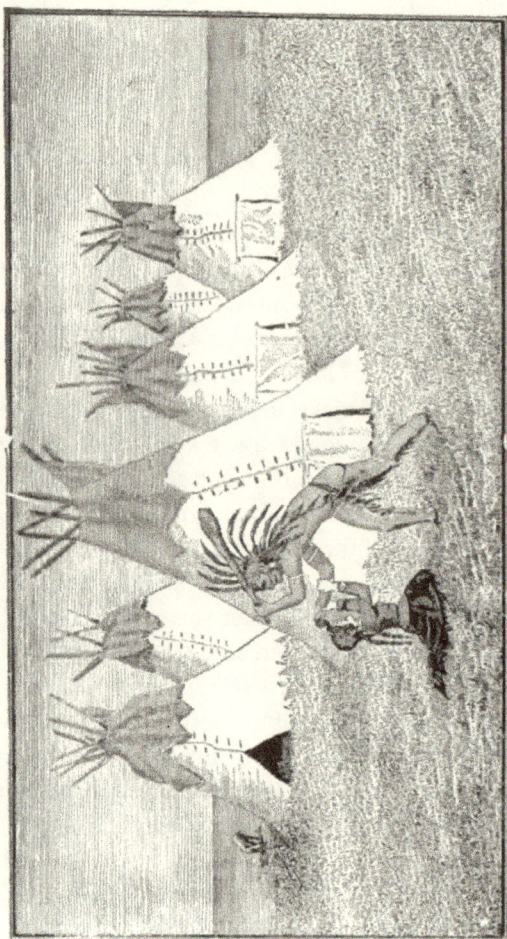

ROARING CLOUD KILLING MRS. NOBLE

force, it was hard for her to submit to their arbitrary and inhuman mandates. Frequently before, she had refused obedience, but in the end was always compelled to submit. All the reward she got for her show of independence was heavier burdens by the way, and a bloody death at last.

No sooner did she positively refuse to comply with Roaring Cloud's demand, than, seizing her by the arm with one hand, and a great stick of wood, she had a little while before brought in for fuel, in the other, he dragged her from the tent. When I saw this I well knew what would follow. It would have been madness, and in vain, for me to interfere; the Yankton did not, except by words. I could only listen in silence to the cruel blows and groans, as the sounds came into the tent; expecting he would return to serve me in the same manner. He struck her three blows, such as only an Indian can deal, when, concluding he had finished her, he came into the tent, washed his bloody hands, had a few high words with the Yankton, and lay down to sleep.

The piteous groans from my murdered companion continued for half an hour or so—deep, sorrowful, and terrible; then all was silent. No one went out to administer relief or sympathy, or even out of curiosity. She was left to die alone, within a few feet of those she had faithfully served, and of one by whom she was tenderly loved. Gladly would I have gone to her side, but was perfectly paralyzed, and terror-stricken with the sights and sounds around me. I evidently would not have been permitted to leave the tent, and any attempt to do so would, doubtless, have brought upon my defenceless head a like thunderbolt. Mrs. Noble was about twenty years of age, rather tall and slender though of good form and graceful in her manners. She was a member of the Disciples church, and during the dark days of captivity I have frequently heard her sing gospel hymns in praise of Him who rules the universe.

Now I was left alone with these inhuman murderers, with no one to talk to, no one to share with me my sorrow and woe. Oh! how keenly I felt her sad fate and my lonely situation. While all was still in the darkness of night, and the Indians lay sleeping around me in the tent, with an aching heart full to bursting, I buried my streaming eyes in my hands and prayed to God: "Leave me not alone with these cruel savages! God! wilt thou leave me thus alone?" How gladly would I have lain down in *dreamless sleep*, and have *slept the sleep that knows no waking*.

The next morning the warriors gathered around the already mangled corpse, and amused themselves by making it a target to shoot at. To this show of barbarism I was brought out, and compelled to stand a silent witness. Faint and sick at heart, I at length turned away from, the dreadful sight, without their orders to do so, and started off on the day's march, expecting they would riddle me with their bullets; for why should I escape more than others? But for some unaccountable reason I was spared. After going a short distance I looked back, and they were still around her using their knives, cutting off her hair, and mutilating her body.

All this time the whole camp was in confusion. The squaws were dragging down the tent-poles, wrapping the canvass into bundles, packing the cooking utensils, and loading up the dogs. At last the bloody camp was deserted, and the mangled body left lying upon the ground unburied. Her hair—in two heavy braids, just as she had arranged it—was tied to the end of a stick, perhaps three feet long, and during the day, as I wearily and sadly toiled on, one of the young Indians walked by my side and repeatedly slashed me in the face with it; thus adding insult to injury, and wounding my heart even more than my face. Such was the sympathy a lonely, broken-hearted girl got at the hands of the "noble red man."

At the close of the day we went into camp as usual, but during the night I was suddenly awakened to find the camp in the wildest excitement. The tents were being torn down, the one I was in being pulled down over my head. Everything was being made ready for flight; and flee we did as for dear life. The flight was kept up the remainder of that night and the whole of the next day. When they camped the evening after Mrs. Noble's death, the stick to which her hair was tied was stuck into the ground near one of the tents, and was forgotten in the panic of the sudden departure.

The cause of this flight I was unable to determine exactly. The Sioux, being at war with all other tribes of Indians, might have suspected that they were being pursued by their enemies; but as the warriors made no preparation for battle—as when apprehensive of an attack from the soldiers—I concluded that it was some superstitious notion that caused the alarm: perhaps the "spirit of the white woman" they had so wantonly murdered at their last encampment.

It was on the sacred Sabbath that the first scene of this gory drama was enacted. I kept account of the days so as to know when Sabbath came, and in my heart felt the day sacred, no matter what I had to do, or how uncongenial the surroundings might be. Bat now, left entirely alone, with no one to communicate with, I began to lose track of time. At first I had resolved not to do this, but stunned as I was by this last bloody horror, perfectly exhausted with incessant toil, which was now telling upon me more and more every day; and with no one with whom I could pass one word; it is a wonder I did not break down entirely, and a worse calamity befall me than the loss of my reckoning of time.

It was now beautiful spring. Nature was arrayed in her fairest and freshest robes. The prairie, as boundless as the ocean, was decked and beautified with a carpet of various shades of green, luxuriant grass. The trees along the streams put forth their leaves, which quivered on the stems. The birds, decked in their gayest plumage, flitted among the trees, and sang their sweetest songs; while the air was redolent with the perfume of countless flowers. But nature, with all her beauty and glory, had no charms for me, while surrounded with such bloodthirsty savages.

Sadly and wearily the days went by while I was thus down in the very depths of despair. Although with many irregularities, our general course from the Big Sioux was in a north-western direction, leading through the counties of Brookings, Hamlin, and Clark, and into Spink (as now laid out).

We crossed one prairie so vast and so perfectly devoid of timber, that for days not even a hazel-brush, or a sprout large enough for a riding-whip, could be found. The sensation produced by being thus lost, as it were, on the boundless prairie was really oppressive. Exhausted as I was, and preoccupied as my mind was by other things, I still could not ignore the novelty of the situation; and the impressions produced will never be forgotten. As we attained the more elevated points the scene was really sublime. Look in any direction, and the grassy plain was bounded only by the horizon. Then we would journey on for miles, till we reached another elevation and the same limitless expanse of grass lay around us. This was repeated day after day till it seemed as if we were in another world.

I almost despaired of ever seeing a tree again. The only things to be seen, except grass, were wild fowls, birds, buffalo, and antelope. The supply of buffalo seemed almost as limitless as the grass. This was their own realm, and they showed no inclination to surrender it, not even to the Sioux. These, however, waged war upon them daily. They would surround a herd and with clubs kill several before they could escape. There was now no scarcity of provisions. The Indians had a feast every

131

day. They ate all they *could*; and their only grief seemed to be that they could eat no more. Not alone did the warriors feast, but the squaws as well, and even the poor captive had plenty. Not only was the buffalo steak eaten, but the brains, lungs, liver, and blood were greedily devoured, and raw at that. No sooner does a Sioux kill a buffalo than he chops open the head, scoops out the brain, and gobbles it down with the voraciousness of a hungry bloodhound. This was his sweetmeat. If there was any part of the animal preferred before the brain, it was the blood. This he sucked with the avidity of a weasel, not waiting for the animal to die, but gulped it as it flowed. The stomach of the buffalo is emptied of its contents and used as a canteen to carry water in. The horns are made into spoons and coarse combs.

The antelope were not so easily captured. They were both timid and fleet, and here, at least, were by no means so plentiful. They would start up from their coverts, like Fitz James's soldiers from the rocks, and bound away over the prairie, as if on legs of steel, with hoofs and joints of rubber. The antelope is said to be to the American plains what the gazelle is to the African. At least they are graceful in form and movement and literally fleet as the wind.

While journeying through Dakota, we on one occasion passed what had evidently been the scene of a great battle. A large number of scaffolds had been erected by setting in the ground four strong posts, and laying long poles on these, and then laying shorter and lighter ones across. These scaffolds were eight or nine feet high, perhaps fifteen feet long by six wide. The bodies had evidently been laid across the scaffold, and were closely packed, side by side; but when we were there only bones remained. These the winds had blown about until they lay thickly strewed upon the ground.

At this battlefield we halted for perhaps an hour, but did not pitch our tents or prepare food. The Indians seemed greatly interested in the osseous relics, picked them up, exhibited them to each other, and made much talk over them. The skulls especially interested them, and after examining them, and chattering over them, they laid them back upon the scaffolds.

The lighter poles had been blown from some of the scaffolds, but the posts or crotches were yet standing. By whom, and how long since, this great battle was fought I could only conjecture. The posts and poles must have been brought several miles, as there was no timber near. Probably the bodies of the enemy had not been thus cared for, but had been left to rot on the ground, or to be devoured by beasts of prey.

As I could not understand very much of their language, their words and actions were a mystery to me, and perhaps impressed me more profoundly and permanently on that account. I have often wished that I could have learned the historic facts connected with the spot. At the time I was too nearly exhausted, and too much overcome with fear and sorrow, to care much for these things. Possibly the earlier settlers in Dakota territory could tell something of the place, or at least the Indian tradition of it.

CHAPTER 21

Arrival of Rescuing Party

If Mrs. Noble could only have escaped the vengeance of Roaring Cloud a few days longer, she doubtless would have been set at liberty, and restored to civilized society and the companionship of her sister and two brothers. These were living at this time in Hampton Iowa. Could she only have known the efforts being made for her rescue, and how near they already were to success, she would have had courage to endure insults a little longer and hope to bid her look forward. At the very moment when she was dragged from her tent and brutally murdered, rescuers, under the direction of the United States commissioner, fully prepared for her ransom, were pressing forward with all the dispatch possible.

It was only a few days after her death that we reached the banks of the James River, where now is situated the town of Old Ashton, in Spink County, D. T. Here was an encampment of one hundred and ninety lodges of Yanktons, a powerful branch of the Sioux nation. I counted the lodges, and would have been glad to count the Indians had that been practicable. But there were evidently two thousand, or more. All the other Indians I had ever seen seemed tame and civilized by the side of these. There was not a single article of white man's manufacture visible. The *teepes* were made of buffalo robes as was their clothing (when they wore any). They started their fires with flint, and roasted their meat on the fire or ate it raw. Some time previously they had captured some property from the Red River half-breeds, but at this time little or none of it was visible.

Bows and arrows and clubs were their principal weapons. In the use of these they were expert. From fifty to seventy-five of these Yanktons would surround a herd of buffalo, and knock down and kill them by the dozen. They made no use of salt; but the meat, sliced and spread in the sunshine, would dry without becoming tainted. This was a mystery to me then, but I have since learned that it may be done almost anywhere in central North America.

I was probably the first white person these Yanktons had ever seen, and was, to them, as great a curiosity as anything Barnum ever brought out was to the people of civilized communities. They not only gathered around the door of the *teepe* where I was, but came in and looked me over, wondering and commenting on my flaxen hair, blue eyes, and still light, though terribly tanned complexion. Some of my original captors would roll up my sleeves showing my untanned arms, and then explain that when they found me my face and hands were as white as that. No sooner was one company out of the *teepe* than others came; and so they kept it up from morning until night, day after day, as long as I was with them. If my one-legged proprietor had only had an eye to business, and had charged every adult a mink-skin, and children under twelve a muskrat-skin, he might have filled his tent with downy pelts, and possibly have paid his way to the national capital, where he in turn might have been an object of curiosity. At least, if he did not feather his nest, he might have lined it with fur. But, possibly, he felt that to be the owner of such a curiosity was honour enough.

This camp of the Yanktons was located on the west bank of the James River, and unfavourable as my situation was for aesthetic enjoyment, I could not altogether ignore the grandeur of the landscape. The river, though not wide, is deep and clear, and the water dark blue. At intervals along the banks are clumps of thrifty timber, gracefully and copiously festooned with wild grape and other clinging vines. As the river travels on in majestic winding curves and loops, its course may be traced for many miles by these picturesque groups of timber. On either side, the green, rolling prairie is limited only by the horizon.

The rich soil produced grass on which subsisted immense herds of buffalo. All that were slaughtered by the voracious Indians seemed to have no effect towards exhausting 'the supply. But, lo! what a change a few short years have wrought. Where then buffalo, and naked savages who had never seen the face of a white man or learned any of the arts of civilized nations, then subsisted on the spontaneous luxuriance of nature now a teeming population, abreast with the front line of modern progress, culture, and refinement, develops and controls the resources of nature. Spink County has today, (as at time of first publication), a population of not less than 8,000. Two great railroad corporations have extended their lines up the James, and one has pushed a second line well into the county from the east, making over one hundred miles of railway in the county. Such are some of the changes twenty-seven years have wrought in Dakota.

We had been in this camp two or three days, and the novelty and excitement caused by the arrival of Inkpaduta's band, with a white captive, had hardly begun to subside, when a new and to me more intense excitement occurred. By this time all hope of ever escaping this bitter, galling servitude had completely died out. I had once changed masters, it is true; but it brought no relief. We were constantly moving further and further from civilization, and deeper into the heart of an unbroken realm of barbarism. The disappearance of all traces of civilization in manners, customs, clothing, or equipments, told me how widely we were separated from the abode of the whites. The purchase of Mrs. Marble had awakened a little hope, that possibly she would reach the whites, and thus interest might be awakened in my behalf. But we had now tramped one hundred and fifty miles toward the setting sun since she left, and no help or word had come.

Besides, Mrs. Noble and myself had been bought, but were not taken to the whites, and one of us had been cruelly murdered. For aught I knew it might have been no better with Mrs. Marble. But even if she did escape, or reach friends and awaken their sympathy for me, what could they do? I well knew that any attempt to rescue me by force of arms would result in my immediate death. I had no friends, powerful or wealthy, either to move the general government or to plan my rescue through private influence. Despair settled upon me. I had one dear sister, it is true; but at this time I knew not whether she was dead or alive. Mrs. Noble's cruel and unprovoked death had extinguished the last ray of hope. No words can express, or imagination conceive, my situation at this time. Hope gone, physical vitality and energy exhausted, I was bruised, sore, and lame in every part of my body. It seemed impossible for me to get rested. Although twenty-eight years have passed since then, I have not recovered from the fearful strain upon my physical and nervous system.

Of all the living things taken in Iowa and Minnesota, Dr. Harriott's pony and myself were all that remained. Of the seventeen horses taken, all save this one had succumbed to the severity of the journey and the cruelty of their masters. The horses had starved to death, or died from exhaustion, and been eaten by the Indians before grass had come, and while game was scarce.

While this dark cloud of gloom was settling upon me heavier and heavier day by day, a deep interest was being awakened in the hearts of the most influential persons in Minnesota. Among these were Governor Medary and Major C. E. Flandreau. To these persons I owe a debt of gratitude I can never repay. How often have I mentally exclaimed, "Where would I have been, or what would have been my fate, had it not been for these men!" Their well-laid and carefully executed plans are so happily told in Major Flandreau's report (which see), that words of mine are needless.

The morning of May 30th dawned as fair and lovely as any mortal eye has ever seen. The sky was blue, the earth green, the air balmy with the breath of spring; while the sun poured down a perfect flood of golden light. But all the brightness and beauty of nature could not symbolize the brightness of that day to me.

While the Yanktons, as usual, were crowding our tent to see the "white squaw," there came into the tent three Indians dressed in coats and white shirts, with starched bosoms. Coming into the camp of the Yanktons, who were without a single shred of white man's make, these coats and shirts would naturally attract attention and excite wonder. To me the interest was deep and thrilling. I knew, at once, that they were from the borders of civilization, whether I should ever reach there or not; but it was some comfort even to see an Indian clothed in the habiliments of the whites.

Much as I wished to communicate with them, I dared not attempt it. I could only watch and wait. No attempt was made by them to communicate with me, and I was left in doubt as to the object of their visit. I at once discovered, however, that there was some unusual commotion among them, and was not long in divining that it was concerning me. Councils were held after the usual fashion of the Indians. First, they gathered in and around the *teepe* where I was; then, they adjourned to the open prairie, where they sat in a circle and talked and smoked and smoked and talked.

These pipes—though the same as ordinarily used—yet deserve description. The bowls were made of the red pipestone, clumsily wrought, and large enough to hold a good, single handful. The stems were of reed, found abundantly in marshy places, or of ash. They are usually some two feet long, and often ornamented with brass nails. After holding their council for an hour or two, they would walk about and talk and eat, then gather into a circle again. This they kept up for three days, during which time I was kept in perfect ignorance as to the state of affairs. Inkpaduta's men and the Yanktons, however, amused themselves by telling me the most fearful and outrageous falsehoods. The Indians' love of torturing their victims is well illustrated in these falsehoods. Along with other things they told me that the "Indians with *shirts*" were going to take me a long way off, farther from the whites, and where there were a great many more Indians, and that then I would be killed.

As to the method everyone seemed to have a version of his own. One would say that I would be taken to the river and drowned, portraying, with gesture, my gasping for breath, and dying struggles in the water. Another would tell me that I would be bound to a stake and burned, showing the manner in which I would writhe and struggle in the flames. Another declared that I was to be cut to pieces by inches; taking his knife and beginning at my toes, or fingers, he would show how piece after piece was to be cut off, leaving the vital parts till the last, that they might wring from me the last possible groan and the last pang of anguish. To all this I listened with composure and indifference. But the darkest cloud, we are told, has a silver lining, and there is said to be a soft spot in even an elephant's head, though it may be hard to find. The only instance of truth, and the only manifestation of sympathy showed me during my captivity, came in right here.

One day, after the Indians had been describing the fearful things about to befall me, and had gone out, leaving me alone with a Yankton squaw, she took pains to tell me that there was no truth in their "yarns;" but that I was to be taken where there were many whites, and no Dakotas; and that I was to be free again. Which to believe I hardly knew. The squaw seemed to be sincere, and actuated by a generous impulse, but honesty and generosity were such rare virtues among them that I could hardly believe her. On the other hand the adverse statements had been made in the presence of the "Indians in shirts," and had gone unrebuked, as far as I could see: so I was kept in suspense and trepidation, vacillating between hope and fear.

A fellow feeling makes us wondrous kind. At this same time this squaw told me how cruelly her *husband* treated her. She pointed him out as he sat in council; and then would strike herself, to show how he was accustomed to beat her. It was no unusual thing for the males thus to treat the squaws. I have often seen the squaws fleeing from tent to tent, screaming at the tops of their voices, seeking to escape from their infuriated masters.

All this *parley* and these repeated councils, I subsequently learned, were occasioned by the fact that the council was divided. The head

Yankton chief seems to have been something of a "*granger*," and disposed to ignore *middle-men*. He therefore proposed that they should themselves take me to the military station on the Missouri River, claiming that they would get more for my ransom than these Yellow Medicine men were able to pay; that is, more tobacco and powder. At last, however, his consent was obtained, somewhat as the votes of pale-faced legislators have often been. A present was made to him, and then all *went merry as a marriage-bell*.

The price paid for my ransom was two horses, twelve blankets, two kegs of powder, twenty pounds of tobacco, thirty-two yards of blue squaw cloth, thirty-seven-and-a-half yards of calico and ribbon, and other small articles, with which these Indians had been provided by Major Flandreau.

The bargain having been agreed to and the price paid, I was at once turned over into the hands of my new purchasers. But so great a business transaction as this must be sealed and celebrated by nothing less than a dog-feast. Of all feasts known to the Indians a dog-feast is the greatest, and the giving of such a feast to me and my purchasers was the highest honour they could have conferred upon us. I was, however, so unappreciative of the honour, and had such prejudice against dog-soup, that I did the unhandsome thing to remain in my tent. This feast occurred in the after part of the day, and together with the many and mysterious rites and ceremonies connected with it continued well into the night. This was my last night with the Yanktons; one never to be forgotten. I was still in uncertainty, but felt thankful to get rid of those from whom I had suffered so much, and who had murdered so many dear to me.

CHAPTER 22

Returning to Civilization

The next morning after the dog-feast, we left the Yankton encampment early, and with it Inkpaduta and his band. Two Yanktons sons of End-of-the-snake—accompanied us as an escort and safeguard against Inkpaduta or any of his men. It was feared that they might be unwilling for me to be taken back to the whites, and so follow my new masters and kill me, as they had Mrs. Noble. But as the Yanktons were far more powerful than Inkpaduta, and as these two men went with us by the authority of the chief, it would have been dangerous business for them to molest me while thus, as it were, under the safe conduct of the great Yankton chief.

Almost the first move was to cross the James River. Here I was put into a frail little boat, made of buffalo-skin, stripped of hair and dressed, so as to be impervious to water. The boat was not more than five feet long, by four wide, and incapable of carrying more than one person. When I found I was to be the only occupant, I concluded that the story of the Indian, who told me I was to be drowned, was after all the true one. I thought surely I was to be sent adrift and left to my own destruction. I was, however, happily disappointed to see my new purchasers divest themselves of their fine clothes and swim across, holding the end of a cable, made of buffalo hide, which had previously been fastened to the boat. With this they drew the boat, with me in it, to the eastern shore of the James River. Thus, though I knew it not, I was being drawn toward home and friends, and the river was put between me and my cruel foes.

Here, on the bank, I was left in charge of some of our party, while others went after a wagon and span of horses that had been hidden, lest those who held me in captivity should demand them also as part of my ransom. Hiding the team and wagon was not only a piece of sharp practice, but a wise stroke of policy and shrewd diplomacy. These three Indians showed sagacity as well as courage in this enterprise. *When Greek meets Greek then comes the tug of war;* and an Indian understands an Indian, and knows how to manage him.

The names of the persons composing this rescue-party should be put on record, and held in remembrance, not alone for this mission, but for other humane deeds done by them. They were: Mazaintemani, or Man-who-shoots-metal-as-he-walks, but now familiarly known among the whites as John Other Day; Hotonwashta, or Beautiful Voice; and Chetanmaza, or Iron Hawk. They were quiet, intelligent-looking, middle-aged men, and prominent members of the church at the mission-station on Yellow Medicine.

Mazaintemani, who was leader of the expedition, was president of Dr. Riggs's Hazelwood republic, and is represented as possessing much of that oratorical power for which many of the aborigines are celebrated. He not only conducted me safely to the whites, but went with me to St. Paul. He afterwards was taken to Washington, where he had an interview with President Buchanan. Here he fell in love with a "Washington lady," whom he found acting as "waiter" in the dining-room of one of the hotels. This love was reciprocated, and the "waiter" became the wife of the president of Hazelwood republic. During the memorable Minnesota massacre of 1862 he remained faithful to the whites.

Faithful found among the faithless;
Faithful only he.

By so doing he, at one time, saved the lives of sixty-two persons. For his faithful services at this time he was rewarded by the state of Minnesota with one hundred and sixty acres of land. He died, some four or five years ago, (as at time of first publication), of pulmonary consumption.

The Yankton chief having been placated, I safely towed across the river, and the team brought out, the Yanktons filled the wagon with dried buffalo meat, buffalo-robes, etc. I was installed driver, and the five Indians (three Yellow Medicine and two Yanktons) leading the way, in single file, we took up our line of march. Our route led due east, so that every morning the sun rose directly in our faces, until we reached Lac qui Parle Lake on the Minnesota River. At one time, as we were fording a river, Hotonwashta pointed down the stream and said, "Steamboat," and by other signs gave me to understand that we

141

were to have a ride on a steamboat. The statement of the one kind-hearted squaw, the direction we were taking, and the word "steamboat," with accompanying gestures, were all that I had from which to form an opinion as to our destination. There were, however, as we shall see, circumstances tending to confirm the more terrible prophecies of the warriors.

After seven days of incessant travelling through a beautiful country, and with almost uninterrupted pleasant weather, we came into a region thickly peopled with Indians. Some of these were living in log-houses, and when my eye first caught sight of one of them my heart fairly bounded with joy. I thought surely we were nearing the abode of white people. But when I reached the house, and found it inhabited by Indians, my heart was as heavy as before it had been light. The large number of Indians also tended to depress me. I thought the fearful stories of the warriors were true, or that I had only been sold from one tribe to another a little more civilized.

Two days of this suspense brought me to the house of a half-breed who could speak the English language. Here my anxiety was put forever at rest. There were residing at this place two half-breed girls who came to see me, and I accompanied them to their home, which was kept very neat and tidy. Their father was a white man; but their mother was a full-blooded Sioux, in full Sioux costume. She sat on the floor, and would not eat with the family at the table. From them I learned that my purchasers were acting under instructions from the U. S. Indian agent; and that the long journey, with its perils and sacrifices, had been made for me. All my fears from them had been groundless, as they were really my friends. How often it is thus in life, we do not know our friends from our enemies. I also learned, from these half-breeds, that Mrs. Marble had been there about a month before, and had gone on to St. Paul.

These sisters (half-breeds) very kindly made me several presents: among them some very beautiful *moccasins* trimmed with beadwork. But such was my abhorrence of everything that reminded me of the Indians that I threw away the *moccasins* as we crossed the river, a short distance from the house. We stopped at this station a day and a half, during which time, without pattern or model, and of course without sewing machine, I cut and made a full suit of clothing for myself. The style and fit might not have been approved by Worth; but it was *worth* everything to me. I had not time to make a bonnet, and could not get one here; so I entered the first white family bareheaded, as I had gone all these months, through winter's cold and summer's heat.

Inkpaduta's squaws had copiously oiled my hair and painted my head and face deepest red. The paint was applied to my head along the line where the hair parted; to my face on the cheeks, and in lines drawn backward from the corners of my eyes; and whereever it helped to make me look hideous. If we were not on a tramp, they made me sit in the sunshine, bare-headed, for hours at a time, when not at work. Their object for keeping me in the sun I do not know, unless it was to tan my skin, and make me dark like themselves.

When I found that I was soon to be among white people, I began to wash in "dead earnest," to get off the paint and oil; but this was a slow process, and required time. Especially was this true of my hair; but I did my best to get rid of all traces of these hated monsters.

After a day and a half spent at this half-breed's trading post—in which time I had tried to make myself as respectable as possible,—we proceeded to the Yellow Medicine Agency, and then to the mission station of Dr. Thomas S. Williamson. When we reached this agency, a scene of wild confusion met us. It was about time for the annuity Indians to receive their pay from government; but for some reason, not known, there was a delay in receiving their supplies. Major Flandreau had gone to St. Paul to see what the trouble was, and to arrange matters. All the Indians belonging to that agency had come in for their share of the payment, and as no intelligible explanation could be given them for the delay they became very much excited. They conjectured that the annuities were being withheld because of the depredations committed by Inkpaduta's band, and my being there at the time tended to confirm this belief. Their desperate and hostile bearing greatly alarmed the few white people stationed at this point, and they feared another outbreak would be the result. That this was no groundless fear was proved by the massacre of 1862.

Thus my escape began to seem well nigh hopeless. Even at this period I was in danger of being killed, or carried again into captivity.

There had been times when I had lost all fear and dread of death, and all hope of rescue; but now life seemed more precious, and liberty sweet. Why had I been spared so long, I thought, and been brought to the very threshold of liberty, only to be put to still more torture? At no time did I feel the danger of my situation more keenly than now.

These greatly excited, armed, and war-painted Sioux warriors thronged the government building by hundreds, demanding their annuities. At last, after much *parleying* through an interpreter, they were persuaded to await the return of the agent from St. Paul, with the assurance that they would then be paid.

While this dun cloud of war hung over our heads, one of the Yanktons—who had accompanied us as an escort from the James River—brought out a beautiful Indian war-cap, that had been carefully packed away in the wagon without my knowledge. I was seated on a stool in the centre of the room, and with great display of Indian eloquence it was presented to me, and placed upon my head, in the name of the great chief Matowaken. The instructions of the chief were, that I should be crowned with it on our first arrival at the abode of the whites; and that it should be exhibited when we came into the presence of the "Great Father," the governor of Minnesota.

The cap was made in this manner: first, there was a close fitting cap, of finely dressed buckskin, soft and light. Around this was a crest of thirty-six of the very largest eagle-fathers, the quills being set with the utmost exactness, so as to form a true circle, wider at the top than at the base. Around the crest, the cap was covered with weasel fur, white as ermine, while the tails of weasels, equally as white, hung as pendants, all around, except in front. The tips of the feathers were painted black. Then there was a stripe of pink; then of black again; and the rest was pink. When properly adjusted upon the head, it was beautiful. If grand in the estimation of the whites what must it have been in the eyes of the Dakotas? To them, every feather represented the high honour of having slain a fellow-mortal. The strangest thing about it was, that the great Yankton chieftain was willing to part with it. In so doing, he conferred the highest honour known to the Dakotas upon me.

INDIAN WAR-CAP.
From a Daguerreotype taken
at Dubuque, June 26, 1857.

In the presentation speech, it was stated, that it was given as a token of respect for the fortitude and bravery I had manifested; and it was because of this that Inkpaduta's Indians did not kill me. It was also stated that as long as I retained the cap I would be under the protection of all the Dakotas.

The Indians having been appeased by the promise of their annuities, and the excitement being over, we proceeded on our journey, which led down the Minnesota River.

During my stay with Dr. Williamson, the missionary, and his family, I was treated with great kindness and consideration; was furnished with more becoming apparel, than that I had constructed while among the half-breeds; was supplied with a bonnet; etc. Everything was done that possibly could be, to alleviate my sufferings, both mental and physical: Had it not been for this great kindness I should have sunk under a consciousness of my forlorn and helpless situation. As the prospect of being set at liberty grew stronger, and the time nearer, I the more intensely realized that I was a poor, friendless orphan, without so far as I knew a near relative in the world. But just at this time the dear heavenly Father gave me many very kind friends. Not alone at this mission, but all along the journey; and all through the journey of life it has ever been the same. He who declared himself the Father of the fatherless has ever been such to me. The darkest cloud has its silver lining, if not its golden border. Till I had known sorrow, I did not, could not, know sympathy.

CHAPTER 23

Delivered Over to the Governor

The coast being now clear, we again took up the line of march. The wagon and horses, that had brought me all the way from the James River, were now abandoned. A Mr. Robinson took his own team and lumber-wagon, and in company with an interpreter, and the three Indians, we started on. We stopped over Sabbath with the family of a physician at the Redwood or Lower agency, thirteen miles above Fort Ridgley. Here again we were most kindly and hospitably entertained. Their kindness I can never forget; although the name, I am sorry to say, I have forgotten.

Captain Bee, commandant at the fort, learning of my arrival at the agency, sent Lieutenant Murray, with a horse and buggy, to bring me down to the fort, where the others would rejoin me on their way Monday. But the Indians, in the suspiciousness of their nature, believed this to be a device to get me out of their hands without paying them for their trouble, and would not let me go. So we remained over Sabbath, and took dinner at the fort on Monday. Here, also, we were kindly entertained, and many valuable presents were made me. Mrs. Bee gave me a purse containing several dollars in gold, and a beautiful gold ring. Lieutenant Murray took me to a store, where he bought me a shawl and the material for a dress, as fine as was in the store.

In the afternoon we again started on our journey, and soon reached Traverse, then the head of navigation on the Minnesota, or St. Peter's River. Here the prophecy of Hotonwashta that we were to ride on a steamboat proved true. Abandoning the lumber-wagon, we embarked on the steamer bound for St. Paul.

The news of the return of the expedition sent out by Major Flandreau, and the rescue of the "captive," spread over the state like fire over the prairie. A deep interest in our fate had been manifested in

Minnesota from the first, which had been greatly increased by the rescue of Mrs. Marble and her accounts of our sufferings.

My appearance, and that of the rescuing party, together with the story of Mrs. Noble's death,—whose mutilated body the friendly Indians had found, and to which they had given burial,—awakened great indignation toward the Sioux, and sympathy for us.

We reached Shakopee June 22nd. As we halted there, a crowd gathered on the boat and dock, and so great was the sympathy that a purse of thirty dollars was raised for me in a few minutes. On the boat crowds gathered around to hear my answers to questions put by some one of the passengers, and many valuable presents were made me, besides some money. At 6 p. m., June 22, we reached St. Paul. Our coming was known, and crowds and deafening shouts from the people greeted the approach of our boat. A carriage was waiting, and we were conducted at once to the Fuller House, then the leading hotel in the city. I was delivered into the hands of the landlady, by whom I was carefully provided for, and every want anticipated.

At 10 o'clock next morning—Tuesday, June 23—I was formally delivered over to the governor, at his room in the Fuller House, by the three Indians, with much ceremony.

The ample reception-room was filled with a select company of distinguished ladies and gentlemen, among whom were Chas. E. Flandreau, U. S. Indian agent; Wm. J. Cullen, superintendent of Indian affairs; Fletcher Williams, now secretary of the Minnesota Historical Society; Colonel L. P. Lee, of New Britain, Ct.; Mr. and Mrs. Long, of the Fuller House; and other persons of note.

After the Indians had shaken hands with the Governor, Mazaintemani addressed him as follows:

Father:—We have come to the white settlement, not of our own accord, but at the wish of the white people. Our father sent us off on business; we have got through with that business, and have come to meet him here.

The American people are a great people—a strong nation; and if they wanted to could kill all our people, but they had better judgment, and permitted the Indians to go themselves, and hunt up the poor girl who was with the bad Indians. We believed when we left our kindred and friends that we would be killed ourselves; but notwithstanding this we desired to show our love for the white people. Our father could have sent troops

147

after Inkpaduta's band, but that would have created trouble, and many innocent people would have been killed. That was the reason we desired to go ourselves. We have been among the white people a good deal, and have been assured by good traders that the whites would always punish those who had done wrong. Last spring we heard of the troubles about Mankato, and we were very desirous to get among the Indians before the troops in order that innocent blood might not be shed.

The Wapetons and Sissetons made a treaty with the whites, but we are fearful even they will get into trouble. There are good and bad men everywhere—could not point to any nation where all were good. Among the Chippewas, the Sioux of Missouri, and the red half-breeds, there were good and bad men. The Wapetons and Sissetons had sold their lands to the Great Father. He had pity on them and gave them a reserve here to live upon; but they were not well treated always. Indians had dark skins, but yet had five fingers and two eyes, and therefore wanted to be as much respected as the whites. We want to become as industrious and as able to do something for ourselves as the whites are. We have a church, and I attend it every Sunday and hear good advice. We want good counsel.

There were bad Indians, but we desired to behave well. We want this known and considered by our Great Father in Washington. The whites told us to stop making war and lay down the *tomahawk*. The advice was good, and we have followed it; and now our women can plant in peace. We wish to say a word in reference to the Yanktons. For many years they had trouble with the Red River half-breeds. We told them not to fight the Red River men, as they counted themselves as Americans; and they promised us they would not. The Yanktons desired their father should be informed of their determination, and that the Red River men should be made acquainted with their desire for peace.

Our father, the agent, desired us to go out and hunt this poor girl. The Great Spirit had pity on her, and we succeeded in finding her. You see the girl here in the power of the white people. We have acted according to the will of the agent. We now give her up to you, but desire to shake hands with her before leaving.

The above speech was addressed to Governor Medary. Upon its conclusion, Agent Flandreau desired one of the Indians present to give an account of the journey from the Yellow Medicine agency to the camp of the Yanktons, where I was discovered. In accordance with the request, Hotonwashta, or Beautiful Voice, addressed the agent as follows:

Father:—About planting-time you came up, and we started for Inkpaduta's lodges. Had we not been sent out then we would have had a great yield. Four days after we left Yellow Medicine we came to the place where the other woman was killed. We took blankets, wrapped her in them, and buried her. In two days more we got to the camp of the Yanktons; but Inkpaduta had got there two days before us. When we arrived, we offered everything we had for the girl, but the Yanktons refused the first time. We waited four days, and the Yanktons were divided into two parties. One desired to take her to the Missouri and surrender her to the military; and others desired to bring her here. They were about quarrelling when the braves determined to surrender her to us. We slept six nights before we reached the Yellow Medicine. We found you was not there, and we followed you to St. Paul. The girl is yours now. Our conduct shows the heart of the Indian toward the whites. We threw away our lives to benefit the whites, in Inkpaduta's camp; but the Great Spirit had pity on us and preserved us. It shows that the Wapetons are good people. First, two men were sent out, and they brought in one of the captives, (Mrs. Marble,) and other three were sent out, who also brought in one.

Mr. Flandreau addressed the Indians in response. He referred to the excitement that prevailed among the whites in consequence of the Spirit Lake massacre, and to the fact that it was laid at the door of the entire Sioux nation. It was for this reason, and because he knew the Wapetons were loyal and brave, that he asked them to volunteer and go in search of the unfortunate captives, in order that they might establish the fact that they were friendly to the whites, by rendering important services. He knew the Wapetons so well that he was satisfied there would be no difficulty in procuring volunteers. He knew the expedition would succeed, and had always so predicted to the whites. Mr. Flandreau concluded his remarks by addressing the Indians as follows:

HO-TON-WASH-TA, OR BEAUTIFUL VOICE.
From a Daguerreotype taken at St. Paul, June 23, 1857.

You have gone out and done your duty well and nobly, and are entitled to the gratitude of the white people. I am glad you came down here because it gave you an opportunity to see the Father of all the whites in the territory, and to assure him of your love for the whites. For the services you have rendered you will be rewarded to your entire satisfaction. Your Father will start immediately on a journey to Washington, where he will see your Great Father, and be enabled to explain your part in these matters personally to him.

Governor Medary then addressed the Indians as follows:

My Red Children:—I am happy to meet you here because you have been performing a worthy and humane act. You have brought us back this young white girl, who was taken by those whose conduct you disapprove of. We shall endeavour to restore her to the few friends and relatives she has left, for a greater portion of them have been killed. As you have nobly and promptly risked your lives in behalf of this white woman, we hope all good whites will be as ready to succour your friends in their hour of need. I hope that the occasion will result in a renewal of the friendship of whites and Indians, and that it will be always kept alive.

I well understood and appreciated the danger of sending a large body of soldiers, unacquainted with your country, to attempt the rescue of the women taken prisoners. There was danger that friendly Indians would be killed; and that in the end more harm would result even to the captives from such interference. I felt that Inkpaduta and his band should be punished for their crimes; but I believed, and events have shown, that it was better, in order to rescue the women, to send you out. Major Flandreau and yourselves deserve the thanks of the people of Minnesota, and of the entire country, for your prompt, humane, and wise action. Had any other course been adopted the lives of many whites and friendly Indians would have been sacrificed without the accomplishment of so much good.

I hope the friendly Indians will hold no communication whatever with Inkpaduta's band. They are villains and murderers, and by holding communication with them you would get yourselves into trouble with the whites. I hope there will be a lasting peace between the Indians and their white brethren in

Minnesota.

I will convey to the Great Father at Washington an account of the good deeds you have performed, and will urge, in behalf of the whites of this territory, that all engagements entered into with you shall be faithfully carried out. I will say to him that you desire to keep peace, and that it is the desire of the Indians adjoining you, the Yanktons, that peace should be made between them and the Red River half-breeds, and harmony and peace and industry restored along the borders of our territory. These things I will convey to the Great Father. We thank you for restoring the white woman to us; and, if ever red men, women, or children should be placed in such an unfortunate position, we hope to be able to treat them with equal humanity and kindness. In the name of humanity, of Christianity, and of that church you say you attend, and those precepts and counsels you heed, I again return you our thanks. We will take her, and see that you are liberally rewarded for all the trouble and danger you have subjected yourselves to in serving us.

The remarks of the governor and the agent were received by the Indians with their customary gravity and decorum. The usual "*ho*" was the only expression elicited during the speeches.

At the conclusion of the governor's remarks, Major Flandreau again, in behalf of Matowaken, the Yankton chief, presented me with the war-cap, of which I have previously spoken.

After some little conversation about the pay the Indians were to receive for their services, they shook hands with me and took their leave.

I was now free once more. No longer the slave of slaves in the camp of the Dakotas, but a free girl, tenderly cared for, in a rich and populous city. The generous people of St. Paul contributed $500 for my benefit, as they had previously $1,000 for Mrs. Marble, which we both deposited in one of the St. Paul banks subject to our order, drawing interest at three *per cent* a month. But in the great financial crash in 1857, a few months following, this bank failed, and we both lost every dollar of our money.

At 2 o'clock on Tuesday, June 23, the Indians and Agent Flandreau again assembled in the governor's room for the purpose of arranging with the former for the payment of the ransom. The next day the Indians, accompanied by their agent and interpreter, left St. Paul for

Yellow Medicine Agency.

On the 27th of June Major Flandreau paid each of the three Indians $400 for their services in effecting my release, and took the following voucher:

Mazaintemani,

Hotonwashta,

Chetanmaza.

For rescuing Miss Gardner from captivity among Inkpaduta's band of Indians, and for services performed in attempting the rescue of Mrs. Noble from the same Indians, and for all services performed by them in said matter, $1,200.

Received at Sioux Agency, June 27, 1857, of Samuel Medary, Governor of Minnesota.

Mazaintemani, **X** mark.

Hotonwashta, **X** mark.

Chetanmaza, **X** mark.

I certify that the above account is correct and just, and that I have actually, this 27th day of June, 1857, paid the amount thereof.

Charles E. Flandreau.

We witness the payment of said money, and the signature of said Indians.

A. J. Campbell.

Stewart B. Garvie,

Interpreter

Over three thousand dollars were expended by the territory of Minnesota under the governor's and Agent Flandreau's directions in effecting the release of Mrs. Marble and myself.

While at St. Paul, I learned that my sister had escaped, unharmed, the attack on Springfield, had married, and was living somewhere in Iowa.

Wednesday, June 24th, in company with Governor Medary and Colonel Lee, I embarked on the steamer *Galena* for Dubuque, the governor on his way to Washington to lay the facts of the massacre before the government, and to ask that troops might be sent to punish the Indians and give security to the settlers; I in search of my sister, my only near relative. At Dubuque the governor most affectionately bade me farewell, and I never saw him again. Many years ago he passed from earth; but his kindness, at least to *one*, has never been forgotten.

Scarcely could he have shown more genuine sympathy had he been my own father. He even invited me to make my home in his family, and offered to adopt me as his daughter, a proposition I should have accepted, had I not found my sister.

After an eight days' journey by stage I reached Fort Dodge, where I was most kindly welcomed and entertained by the family of Major Williams. Here I learned that my sister, now Mrs. William Wilson, was living with her husband at Hampton, Franklin county.

I remained in the family of Major Williams until my brother-in-law came for me. We reached my sister in the evening of July 5th. This meeting can well be imagined. Since last we met how much of sorrow and terror we both had seen! It was a sad meeting, for inevitably the dead rose up before us. We had parted in the midst of a circle of loved ones. We met here as two torn, bleeding lambs, all that had escaped the wolf's devouring jaws. Twenty-eight eventful years have passed, (as at time of first publication), since that sorrowful meeting with my sister, years that have brought to each of us much of toil, care, and sadness. We then realized that a dark shadow had fallen upon us; but out of this we hoped life's journey would bring us, and the sunshine of other springs revive the buds that had been blasted as by an untimely frost. All this, indeed, might have been, but for a more subtle and relentless foe, which annually sends to premature graves one hundred thousand of our people, while it enslaves and tortures tenfold more.

Here, at Hampton, in the mysterious order of Providence, it was my sad privilege to convey to the heart-stricken husband, parents, and relatives of Mrs. Thatcher the tender message, so hastily given me, as she was about to tread that fatal bridge, from which she landed on the eternal shore.

Upon his return to his home in Connecticut, Colonel Lee, who accompanied Governor Medary and myself to Dubuque, published an account of the massacre, the material for which was obtained from the author of this volume. From his pamphlet I will be pardoned for making the following extracts:

> It is no easy matter for us who have never seen death in his most savage forms, never lived in scenes of bloodshed, never suffered from privation and want, never braved the rough-and-tumble life of the prairie, or dared the war-whoop and scalping-knife, to realize fully the horrors described in the following pages. Had they transpired in New York or any of our more populous

cities, they would have kindled the sympathies of the whole nation, and excited a worldwide interest. The daily papers would have trebled their circulation while magnifying every incident connected with the "Horrible Tragedy." Every act, every word, every look of the savage perpetrators of such outrages would be reported to thousands of eager readers. Social circles would for weeks talk or think of nothing else. The streets, the hotels, the saloons, the thoroughfares of business, the steamboats, railcars, and in short every resort of the living would ring with the interesting gossip relating to the barbarous massacre.

Miss Abbie Gardner would become a heroine of the most enviable notoriety. Throngs would press to behold her expressive face; crowds would be anxious to know every word that might escape from her lips for months, and she, with all her relatives and fellow-sufferers, would at once take rank among the historical characters of the age. Human hearts vibrate most with sympathy when near the exciting cause, but, like the gently rippling waters far off from the falling stone, they are very slightly moved by the troubles of those at a distance.

Accordingly, we at the east have felt, comparatively, but little sympathy in the Spirit Lake Massacre, while wrath and sympathy have lashed the hearts of our Western countrymen with a tempest of excitement, the surging swells of which are still heard moaning their solemn dirge. Who that gazes upon Miss Gardner's well-formed features, sees the depths of her eyes, the character and strength of endurance and of self-command, and yet the almost enslaved submissiveness, the despairing indifference to fate, the keen suffering and grief, all stamped on her countenance, and shaded by the tawn of her ruthless captors, can read the soul-harrowing tale of her tortures, without a tear of sympathy for the afflicted maiden, and an unutterable feeling of indignation against her foul tormentors?

As children, we have all read with exciting interest the story of the attacks of the Indians on the early settlers of our country. We have felt for the distracted family of Mr. Williams, of Deerfield, Massachusetts, execrated the barbarities committed by the Indians upon Saratoga, and upon the early settlers in Virginia, wept over the bloody murder of Miss McCrea, the luckless victim of Wyoming, and followed with tears and admiration the fortunes of Daniel Boone and his brave companions in Kentucky; but we doubt whether among all these bloodier tomahawks ever gleamed than those which hewed down the settlers at Spirit Lake, or greater fortitude was ever exhibited than that which so heroically shines in Miss *ABBIE GARDNER.*

If misfortune comes she brings along the bravest virtues.—Thompson.

On Wednesday, June 24, 1857, on board the steamer *Galena*, Miss Gardner embarked in company of Governor Medary and Colonel Lee, for Dubuque, Iowa, on her way in search of her only remaining relative, her sister Eliza, who (it will be remembered) was absent, near Fort Dodge at the time of the massacre, and thus escaped. On parting with his young and interesting charge the governor was so touched with her subdued grief, and the intolerable trials she had so meekly and patiently borne, that his eyes filled with tears, in which others present joined, showing much sympathy and feeling for her.

No radiant pearls, which crested Fortune wears,
No gem that twinkling hangs from Beauty's ears;
Not the bright stars, which Night's blue arch adorn;
Nor radiant Sun, that gilds the vernal Morn;
Shines with such lustre as the tear that flows
Down virtue's manly cheek for others woes.

Colonel Lee, at the request of the governor, very gladly undertook the escort of the released captive from Dubuque to Fort Dodge. The governor's parting charge was that if her only surviving sister could not be found, and no other provision made for her, Colonel Lee should take her to Columbus, Ohio, where the governor's family reside, and commit her to the care of Mrs. Medary, who would adopt her and educate her as her own. Through this whole affair, the governor acted with a manliness and discretion as rare as they are admirable.

During this agreeable trip, Colonel Lee enjoyed the interesting society of Miss Gardner for eight days before arriving at Fort Dodge. First to him of all the whites she had seen since her release, she told the details of her wonderful adventures, as they have been narrated in these pages.

While in Dubuque they had been entertained very hospitably by a private family, where an intelligent and well-educated young lady was visiting; she kindly wrote out for Colonel Lee the following description of Miss Gardner as she appeared at that time:

> For a girl of her years, Miss Gardner is rather tall and slender, though with a look of health and endurance. Her manners are quiet and pleasing, and her face, though so deeply browned from her long continued exposure, has a subdued and pensive expression, sufficiently attesting the suffering she has passed through. She has evidently great amiability of disposition, and to this she doubtless owes not only her life, but her exemption from many of the cruelties to which Mrs. Noble, and those who evinced more spirit, were constantly subjected. She seems, even now, to entertain no feelings of wrong, but only of deep thankfulness that she has been rescued from that bondage, in which she had looked forward to death as the only release, and, as we might suppose, longed for its coming.
>
> She speaks of her own suffering with a calmness amounting to indifference, when compared with the depth of feeling she evinces when the dreadful fate of her family is alluded to, and it is then her woman's heart is more manifest than in speaking of any personal abuse she has received. Her complexion is naturally light, with soft blue eyes, and brown hair; but the barbarous manner in which the squaws were accustomed to dressing it was in accordance with our ideas neither of cleanliness nor beauty. They bestowed an abundance of oil from any animal they happened to have killed, and then braided it closely, allowing it to remain for days in this filthy condition, with the full force of the sun's rays burning it into her head, for she wore no protection over her head during the whole of her wanderings.

On arriving at Fort Dodge with his ward, Colonel Lee left her under the care of Major W. Williams. The major promised to provide her as early a passage as possible to her sister when found. In St. Paul Miss Gardner had heard a rumour that her sister had married, and had sent messengers to Minnesota to seek for her. But not until after her arrival at Fort Dodge could she learn where her sister had settled, nor whom she had married.

After leaving her with Major Williams, in Fort Dodge, Colonel Lee learned at Iowa Falls, on his return toward Dubuque, that the object of their search (Miss Abbie's sister) had married Mr. Wilson, and was living at Hampton, in Franklin County, Iowa. The colonel immediately wrote to Major Williams, and also to Mr. Wilson, informing the latter of Miss Gardner's release and stay at Fort Dodge, and the former of his discovery.

CHAPTER 24

Since the Captivity

Among the many relatives of Mesdames Noble and Thatcher residing at Hampton, was a cousin, a young man by the name of Casville Sharp, with whom I naturally soon became acquainted. The acquaintance rapidly became more intimate, and on the 16th of August, 1857, we were married.

Some eighteen months afterwards, in company with my husband, I visited the lakes, the scene of my anguish and unutterable sorrow. Not even the desolation Inkpaduta had wrought could deter people from seeking homes in this charming country. Already the tide of immigration was pouring in. As early as the 15th of April, 1857—only a month after my capture, J. S. Prescott and W. B. Brown arrived: Prescott taking possession of my father's home and claim.

Prominent among those who came in early after the massacre to establish homes, may be mentioned: Henry Barkman, O. C. Howe, B. F. Parmenter, R. N. Wheelock, C. F. Hill, R. Kingman, A. Kingman, Geo. E. Spencer, (since U. S. senator from Alabama,) his brother, Gustave Spencer, M. A. Blanchard, S. W. Foreman, A. Arthur, Dr. Hunter, S. Thornton, E. Parmer, R. A. Smith, his father and brother Milton. Howe, Wheelock, and Parmenter, (as stated in a previous chapter,) had located prior to the massacre, and were among the first to discover the fact; and they assisted in burying the dead.

My object in going to the lakes was to visit the graves of those so dear to me, to add some tribute of affection; and also to secure, if possible, some compensation for the property, and pre-emption claim, of my father, of which possession had been taken by Mr. Prescott. After some delay, I secured a *small* amount, not so much as the personal property left by the Indians was worth, or the improvements made, or the value of the choice location; not so much, in fact, as the old log house would be worth to me today; but it was all Mr. Prescott was willing to pay, and so it was all I could get. While we were there, an intense excitement was raised on account of the reports of the presence of hostile Indians in the vicinity.

One man came in and reported that he had been shot at by an Indian. The next day a small party of Indians was discovered approaching the town. They were halted a short distance from the place, and I went out to see if they belonged to Inkpaduta's band. Had I recognized any of them the citizens stood ready to shoot them down. As they were not the marauders, they were allowed to depart; but they were not permitted to enter the town, as they were believed to be spies trying to find out the situation of the settlers.

United States soldiers had been ordered to the lakes to give security to the settlement for the winter, and were expected soon. In the meantime, the citizens stood guard at night, and for days nothing was thought of, or talked of, but the Indians. With my own terrible experience yet so fresh in memory, and so vividly recalled by the present surroundings, this excitement was unutterably dreadful, and it was with a sense of great relief that I left the place where I had witnessed such bitter scenes of agony and bloodshed, and where I was living in fear of seeing them repeated upon myself and those around me.

Returning again to Hampton, we passed on to Bremer county, where my husband owned land, and where his parents resided. Here, in 1859, came to our home a darling baby boy, whom I called Albert, for my sister's Albert, who was torn from my arms on that memorable day of the massacre.

Most of the time since, I have been a resident of Iowa. Twice we removed to Grundy County, Missouri. The first time we remained only a few weeks; the second time a year. This time it was our misfortune to be burned out of house and home. As we were away when it burned, we lost all the house contained, including not only much valuable property, but also the beautiful war-cap, the relic of my captivity.

Soon afterwards, we moved to Kansas, arriving there just at the time of the great drouth of 1860. This drouth was so severe that on the 4th of July the corn standing in the field was dry as tinder, and the leaves would break into pieces in the hands. The grass was, to all appearances, dead, and would crack under the feet as one walked. The wind blew steadily from the south, and seemed like the air from an oven. We were compelled to remain in the house, and to close the doors and windows, to protect ourselves from the scalding breath of this American *sirocco*.

Great was our disappointment, after journeying so far, to be obliged to leave Kansas at the end of one week. However, to us at least, considerable as was the expense of the journey, the drouth was doubtless a blessing in disguise, as it drove us back to Iowa just in time to escape the ravages of war that for four years swept over that part of the state.

In 1862 I was blessed with the second son. This one we called Allen. He and Albert are both now in the employ of the M. & St. Louis railway company, (as at time of first publication). From Bremer County we removed to Shell Rock, in Butler County, where, in 1870, it was again our misfortune to lose all our household effects by fire. This time, as before, we were away from home, and nothing was saved. In 1871 little Minnie came, but her mission on earth was soon accomplished, and her short life was over in eighteen months. This sorrow was to me the greatest since my captivity.

In 1876 I went East, accompanied by my son Allen, spending some six months in the state of New York, and about the same time in Pennsylvania, visiting among places of interest many of the spots dear to my childhood. Pleasant it was to linger amid the scenes of earlier years; and yet how sad!

Rev. F. M. Smith, my mother's brother, was pastor of the M. E. church at Greenwood, our former home. The stone schoolhouse in which I first attended school, and around which I played, stood just across the stream from this church. The old schoolhouse had been replaced by another, of like material, but larger and better. My uncle's dwelling was only a few rods away, and from his door I could see the children at play, as others and myself had played, more than twenty years before. I could not but think of my own happy life when I played on that same ground, and contrasted it with the years of suffering and sorrow that had followed. I thought of the time when we dwelt there an unbroken family, and the sad fate that befell us by exchanging our home here for one of hardships and privations on the extreme frontier. How could I suppress a sigh or help but wish that we had been content with our home in the Empire State.

Among those whom I visited was Mrs. Lydia Ersley, my first teacher, and ever-remembered friend. Many other places and persons, dear to me, I was not permitted to visit on account of ill health.

Never have I recovered from the injuries inflicted upon me while a captive among the Indians. Instead of outgrowing them, as I hoped to, they have grown upon me as the years went by, and utterly undermined my health. For fourteen years I have been an invalid confined to my room; often, for months at a time, perfectly helpless. For nearly three years I was under the personal care of W. H. Pettit, M. D., of Cedar Falls, Iowa, and it is due to his skilful treatment that I have so far recovered my health, as to be able to prepare this volume. But for the failure of my health this work would doubtless have been given to the world years ago; but perhaps the delay is more than compensated for by greater accuracy in detail.

Many of the publications I have read, touching the events recorded in this history, are so inaccurate and unreliable that I have been constrained, on this account, to give to the public the *facts* as I *know* them to be.

In 1883 I visited St. Paul, where I had not been since that memorable visit *twenty-six* years before, when I was brought there under Indian escort, still held in their custody till the price of my ransom should be paid. One object of my last visit was to gather material for this volume. In this I was most successful, as every facility was offered me. Judge Flandreau put into my hands all his private papers that would throw any light upon this subject. I also had access to all the documents in possession of the State Historical Society, which are very full and complete. The old capitol had fallen a victim to the flames; and many valuable records were destroyed; but, fortunately for me, those pertaining to this history had escaped.

Among the relics shown me at the capitol was the scalp of Little Crow, the great Sioux chief, who claimed to have punished Inkpaduta's band, and who originated, and led in, the scheme to massacre all the whites in the valley of Minnesota. As I turned over the scalp, it was a satisfaction to know that he could never again lead his warriors on to murderous deeds. Had Inkpaduta's scalp been taken, the Minnesota massacre of 1862 might have been averted.

CHAPTER 25

Retribution

About the time I reached Hampton, in 1857, Major Flandreau received the startling news that Inkpaduta and several of his band were on the Yellow Medicine, not far from the agency. The major went to Fort Ridgley to consult with Colonel Alexander as to what ought to be done, and how to do it. They agreed that something ought to be done, to punish the reckless marauders. A lieutenant and eighteen men were detailed to co-operate with Major Flandreau. This work fell to the lot of Lieutenant Murray, of Captain Bee' company,—the same who had made the terrible winter campaign to Springfield, and who had once been so near Inkpaduta and his *desperados*.

He marched his men up to Redwood Agency, a distance of thirteen miles, where he arrived about 5 p. m. Here the major had wagons to transport them to the Yellow Medicine, thirty miles farther. The major had also raised a squad of volunteers to accompany the soldiers.

Several young men were visiting at the agency at the time, who joined the expedition. Among them was a son of Professor Morse, (inventor of the telegraph,) who had been in the military school at West Point. There were in the company three brothers of the name of Campbell; James Maynaer, who afterwards fell leading a company in the war to put down the rebellion; Charles Jenny, who had been a great traveller; and some half dozen more whites and half-breeds. It was arranged to have a guide meet them, to conduct them to the place where Inkpaduta's men were supposed to be. With these preparations they set out about dark.

The Redwood and Yellow Medicine enter the Minnesota from the west, flowing in nearly parallel lines, with a distance of twenty miles between them. The country between is a level prairie with a conspicuous butte, or elevation, about half way from river to river.

This butte is renowned for being the place of a great, four days' battle between the Sioux and Chippewas. The rifle-pits made by the Sioux were still well defined a few years ago, and probably are at this time, (as at time of first publication). From the top of this hill, the timber on both rivers is distinctly visible.

When the expedition reached this butte, on the summit sat John Other Day, whom Joseph Brown had sent as guide to the camp of Inkpaduta. It will be remembered that this guide was one of the party that rescued me. He was sitting, pipe in his mouth, and, Indian like, showed not the slightest sign of interest or recognition, but waited to be spoken to.

He stated that there were some of Inkpaduta's men on the Yellow Medicine, how many he did not know; but could point out their camp. This he described as composed of six *teepes*, standing aloof from all the others, and up the river some five miles from the agency. When asked how they could distinguish Inkpaduta's men from the others, he replied:

> You charge on the camp. When they see the soldiers they will know what they are after. Inkpaduta's people will either run or show fight. The others will remain quiet.

Joe Campbell, the interpreter, approved the wisdom of the advice. The officers decided to capture or kill any who fled, and take the chances of their being the right ones. With this arrangement they moved forward, piloted by Other Day. They reached the river, where they were to cross, just in the gray of the morning. The camp they sought was in sight on a high plateau, north of the river, and about a mile above the ford. The utmost caution had been observed, even before they reached the river, by creeping along, and keeping a knoll of the prairie between them and the camp. The alertness and skill with which Other Day led the expedition, and his snake-like movements, were marvellous. No panther ever stole upon its prey with more dead-ly silence and certainty. The river was about a quarter of a mile from the camp, and forty feet below, with a precipitous bank, which was lined with a thick growth of willow. It was evident that if the Indians ran they would make for the river.

Lieutenant Murray commanded the infantry while the cavalry was under direction of Major Flandreau. The plan of operations was as fol-lows: the infantry were to charge, at double quick, up along the river, and endeavour to cut off a retreat to the cover of the bank; while the cavalry were to keep to the right, and so surround the camp. When all was ready, the word of command was given, and off they started. The night had been sultry, and the *teepes* were rolled up from the bottom for ventilation, thus giving those within an opportunity to observe what was going on without.

A dozen horsemen furiously galloping toward one side of the camp, and fifteen or twenty soldiers charging at double quick toward the other side, could not remain long unnoticed. When they were within about half a mile of the camp, an Indian, holding a squaw by the hand, sprang from one of the *teepes* and darted, like an antelope, in the direction of the river. Other Day and Campbell at once shouted "That's our man!" and rifles began to crack. The soldiers opened on him at long range, as they were somewhat in the rear, and several shots were fired by the mounted men. Whether he was hit or not no one knew, except from the fact that he bounded forward the faster. He had a double-barrelled shot gun in his hand, but did not stop to use it until he reached cover. Here he could not be seen but had full view of his pursuers.

The situation was critical. Every moment a fatal shot was expected. He fired four times, one bullet striking the cartridge-box of one of the soldiers, (which he had drawn to his left side for convenience in loading,) turning it inside out, and destroying all his ammunition. The other shots missed. At each discharge of his gun, a volley was fired at the point where the flash was seen. He was soon riddled with bullets, and as no more shots came a soldier rushed forward and finished the work with a thrust of his bayonet. So fell Roaring Cloud, son of Inkpaduta. His two companions were thought to have fled to the haunts of the old chief.

The soldiers captured the squaw, put her in one of the wagons brought to convey the soldiers, and started down the river for the agency. Their object in taking the squaw was to learn who the Indian was, that had been killed, and to get any other desirable information; but they had not counted the cost of making her a prisoner, as events soon showed.

Three members of Inkpaduta's band had evidently come to the vicinity of the agency, hoping to share in the annuities soon to be dispensed by government; but while looking after rations one, at least, had thoughts of love. This was Inkpaduta, junior, son of the old chief, and Mrs. Noble's murderer, one of the worst of the band. Having triumphed in war, he must now try his skill in love, where he seems to have met with equal success; perhaps successful because of his bloody deeds. Nor, if so, would this be the first time in the history of the world that sacrifices to the god of war seemed to please the gentle goddess of love.

But, having slain his hecatombs upon the altar of Mars, he now lays, not his heart only, but unwittingly his head, upon the altar of Venus. Available and attractive brides seemed to have been wanting in his own band, nor would one of the artless maidens in the Yankton encampment, though arrayed in all the simplicity of nature, meet the demand of this prospective chieftain. He must have a maiden, who was a ward of the United States, and had learned some of the blandishments of civilization. So he woos and wins a bride from among the annuity Indians at Yellow Medicine Agency.

The making prisoner of this fair young widow seemed to have touched the hearts of the Yellow Medicine braves, even more than the sudden "taking-off" of her illustrious husband. In going down to the agency, the expedition passed through the camp of some ten thousand Indians. Here they found they had stirred up a hornet's nest. The excitement was awful. The squaws howled, as only squaws can howl. The warriors, naked, painted, and ready, armed for a fight, scowled, frowned, and swarmed on every side, like an infuriated swarm of bees. A single shot, from either party, would have been as a spark of fire in a magazine, and the little band would have shared a fate like that which in later years overtook Custer and his men. Fortunately no collision occurred, and they reached the agency in safety. Here they took possession of a log house, and awaited results, determined to fight, if need be, while a man could lift a weapon.

The Indians brought up the dead body and held a long council over it. Many speeches were made, similar, in their object, to that made by Mark Antony over the dead body of Caesar; but either there was no "plain, blunt man" with the skill of Antony among them, or else a wholesome fear of the proximity of reinforcements of soldiers restrained them.

Within the little fort were fifty determined men, well organized, with Charles Jenny and young Morse acting as lieutenants. Had an attack been made, there, would have been more than one dead Indian outside. After several days spent in sleepless anxiety, they were reinforced by the arrival of Major Sherman, with the famous Buena Vista battery, who had been ordered up from Fort Snelling to attend the payment of the annuities. Sherman had sixty men with him, which made the little fort a pretty strong garrison, and with the artillery rendered the situation quite safe. They were, however, finally and effectually relieved by several companies of soldiers under Major Patton, who was on his way to Fort Ridgley from some post on the Missouri, and whose coming was most opportune.

The government required, of the Sioux, the delivery of Inkpaduta and his band, as the condition of the payment of the annuities. This the Indians considered as a great wrong visited upon the innocent, for the crimes of the guilty. Notwithstanding, Major Flandreau succeeded in organizing a company of warriors, from each of the different bands of the annuity Sioux, under the chieftainship of Little Crow, numbering in all one hundred and six, besides four half-breeds. This expedition left Yellow Medicine July 22, going out after Inkpaduta. After an absence of thirteen days, they returned, claiming that they had killed three of his band, wounded one, and taken two squaws and one *papoose* prisoners.

In a council held at Yellow Medicine, in August, 1857, by the Sisseton and Wapeton bands of Sioux, one of their speakers, Mazaintemani, said:

> The soldiers have appointed me to speak for them. The men who killed the white people did not belong to us, and we did not expect to be called to account for the people of another band. We have always tried to do as our Great Father tells us. One of our young men brought in a captive woman. I went out and brought in another. The soldiers came up here, and our men assisted them to kill one of Inkpaduta's sons at this place. Then you [Supt. Cullen] spoke of our soldiers going after the rest. Wakeaska [White Lodge] said he would go, and the rest of us followed. The lower Indians did not get up the war-party for you; it was our Indians, the Wapetons and Sissetons.
>
> The soldiers, here, say they were told by you that a thousand dollars would be paid for killing each of the murderers. Our Great Father does not expect us to do these things without money. I suppose it is for that, the special agent [Major Pritchette] is come up. We, with the men who went out, want to be paid for what we have done. Three men were killed as we know. All of us want our money very much. We have not seen our Great Father, but we have heard a great deal from him, and have always tried to do as he told us. A man of another band

has done wrong, and we are to suffer for it. Our old women and children are hungry for this. I have seen $10,000 sent here to pay for our going out. I wish our soldiers were paid for it. I suppose our Great Father has more money than this.

Supt. Cullen replied to a part of this speech as follows:

The money that man saw was the annuity moneys. I have never promised a thousand dollars a head, or any other sum. I have never made an offer for the head of any man. I was willing to pay a thousand dollars, out of my own pocket, to the Indians, if they went and did as their Great Father desired. I know what I say, and I will do as I say. I put my words down when I go home.

Major Pritchette, the special government agent, thought it necessary to answer some other point made by Mazaintemani, and addressed him in council, as follows:

Your Great Father has sent me to see Supt. Cullen, and to say to him that he is well satisfied with his conduct; because he had acted according to his instructions. Your Great Father had heard that some of his white children had been cruelly and brutally murdered by some of the Sioux nation. The news went on the wings of lightning from the extreme north to the land of eternal summer, throughout which his children dwell. His young men wish to make war on the whole Sioux nation, and revenge the death of their brethren. But your Great Father is a just father, and wishes to treat all his children alike, with justice. He wants no innocent man punished for the guilty. He punishes the guilty alone. He expects those missionaries, who have been here teaching you the laws of the Great Spirit, have taught you this.

Whenever a Sioux is injured by a white man, your Great Father will punish the white man; and he expects from your chiefs and warriors of the great Sioux nation that they will punish those Indians who injure the whites. He considers the Sioux as a part of his family, and as friends and brothers he expects them to do as the whites do to them. He knows the Sioux nation is divided into bands; but he also knows how they can all band together for common protection. He expects the nation to punish those murderers, or to deliver them up. He expects this because they are his friends. As long as these murderers are not punished or delivered up, they are not acting as friends of the Great Father. It is for this reason that he has withheld the annuity. He has instructed Supt. Cullen so to say, and so to act.

If you have determined not to punish them or deliver them up, your Great Father will send his own warriors to do so, and he wants no assistance from you. If your father (Supt. Cullen) is satisfied that you will do nothing farther, then the warriors of your Great Father will go out, and if the murderers do not hide in holes like foxes your annuity will soon be paid. Your Great Father will have his white children protected; and all who have told you that he is not able to punish those who injure them will find themselves bitterly mistaken. Your Great Father desires to do good to all his children, and will do all in his power to accomplish it; but he is firmly resolved to punish all who do wrong.

It will be seen by the preceding speeches that the Sioux, under the nominal lead of Little Crow, argued that they had pursued Inkpaduta, killed three of his men, and taken two squaws and one papoose prisoners, and that they had done enough to merit the payment of their annuities. We will only say, that it was the opinion of some of the Indian officials, and the general, intelligent sentiment of the people of Minnesota at the time, that the apparently friendly disposition of the Sioux nation should not be endangered by subjecting them to wants, incident to their present condition, thus leading them into temptation and to commit depredations to which the withholding their annuities might leave them exposed; and that their annuities might now be paid without violating the spirit of the expressed determination of the department, to withhold them until the murderers should be surrendered or punished.

The officials finally yielded this point in favour of the Indians, for the reasons stated: simply because it was thought the best policy. But it was believed by some, and more recent events have greatly strengthened this belief, that, had our government enforced the surrender or the entire extirpation of Inkpaduta's murderous outlaws, the ever-to-be-remembered massacre of August, 1862, would never have happened.

August 18, 1857, Major Cullen telegraphed to Hon. J. W. Denver, Commissioner of Indian Affairs, as follows:

If the department concurs, I am of the opinion that the Sioux of the Mississippi have done all in their power to punish or surrender Inkpaduta's band, and their annuities may with propriety be paid, as a signal to the military movements from Forts Ridgley and Randall. The special agent awaits answer to this dispatch at Dunleith, and for instructions in the premises.

Suffice it to say, the government paid the Indians their annuities, and made no further effort to bring to punishment the remainder of the band, who had escaped the pursuit of Little Crow. The result was that the Indians construed this as an evidence of weakness, or that the whites were afraid to pursue the matter further, lest it should terminate in still more disastrous results to themselves. From this time the Indians on the border of Minnesota became more and more insolent. It is said that Little Crow boastfully declared, that if Inkpaduta with his little band of fourteen warriors could massacre a whole settlement, and create a panic that drove thousands from their homes, and escape unpunished, he, numbering his warriors by thousands, could massacre and expel all the whites from the valley of the Minnesota.

In August, 1862, during our civil war, the cunning, treacherous Little Crow, taking advantage of the troubled condition of the country, attacked the settlers in Minnesota, killing men, women, and children. Not less than eight hundred persons fell victims at this time to savage cruelty. This outbreak was sudden and unexpected, and again consternation swept along the northern boundary of Iowa, while a large portion of Minnesota was depopulated.

On the morning of August 22, 1862, a Norwegian named Nelson came to Spirit Lake, with his two children, that he had carried in his arms from his home on the Des Moines, some fourteen miles north of the Iowa line. On the evening before, the settlers in his neighbourhood had held a meeting to adopt some measures for defence, in view of the reports which had come to them of the Indian depredations at New Ulm. Those who attended the meeting on the evening of August 21st, returned to their homes to find their families murdered and their houses plundered. Nelson found his family all killed except the two children mentioned, and they had been left for dead. One of them afterward died from its injuries, but the other recovered.

These reports caused intense excitement at Spirit Lake, and a party was sent to the Des Moines. They made a hasty reconnoissance, and returned next day, when a larger force was organized and sent over to Jackson, Minnesota, where they were met by another party from Estherville, Iowa. The two parties united, and followed up the Des Moines fifteen miles, where they encamped for the night. About fifteen bodies were found and buried. The next day each party returned to their homes.

The settlers about the lakes immediately gathered at the court-house, and for the time being adopted that as headquarters. A stockade was constructed of boards set up endwise in a trench around the court-house, a distance of twenty feet from it. This was occupied as a military station until 1865; but fortunately no other use of it was required.

CHAPTER 26

Visit to the Old Home

On the tenth day of December, 1883, I made my third journey to Spirit and Okoboji Lakes, not with "prairie schooner," and slowly moving train of oxen, camping out at night, as on my first visit, nor yet with nimble horses, as on my second; but with steed of iron, whose nerves were steel and whose breath was flame, we flew over the prairie with the speed of the wind. The landmarks we then looked forward to with anxious longing, and toward which we patiently toiled, now fled backward as the train sped on.

But not more changed was the mode of conveyance than were the objects that met our eyes. Where then stretched the trackless prairie as far as the eye could see, were now fields, barns, stacks of grain, and commodious dwellings. How different the scene since 1856 and 1858, when last I beheld these shores. The groves and hills which once echoed with the war-whoop of the savages now reverberates with the shrill whistle of the locomotive. Now, upon the western shore of the north end of East Okoboji, about one and a half miles from Spirit Lake, deriving its name from the latter, we beheld a promising young city, with all the advantages and conveniences of advanced civilization, the county-seat of Dickinson County, and the junction of two great railroads—the Burlington, Cedar Rapids & Northern, and the Chicago, Milwaukee & St. Paul—connecting it directly with the great centres of population and trade.

One great improvement worthy of note, that has been wrought where a few years ago might have been seen the *wigwams* of the Dakotas, is the Hotel Orleans, the pride of Spirit Lake, with its half mile or more of verandas, and its nine artistic towers, furnishing ample room for hundreds of observers to behold the magnificent scenery of the surrounding country. This hotel is beautifully located on the isthmus between Spirit Lake and East Okoboji. It was built, and is owned, by the B., C. R. & N. railway company, and is said to be the largest in the state, (as at time of first publication).

Five miles south of Spirit Lake, on the Chicago, Milwaukee & St. Paul railway, and also on the strait connecting the two Okobojis, is the town of Okoboji, with a neat and beautiful depot-building, steamboat-landing, post-office, store, etc. On the north side of the strait, near the spot where the Granger cabin stood, is now a large residence owned by Mr. Smith, one of the early settlers.

On the south side of the railroad bridge, and within a few rods of the lake shore, is the place where the helpless Mattocks perished in the flames of their own dwelling, and where I spent that never-to-be-forgotten night of horrors the first of my captivity; where, in the hideous orgies of the war-dance, Inkpaduta's bloody warriors celebrated the slaughter of my kindred. On the claim of my brother-in-law, Mr. Luce, half a mile southwest of this, and by the path over which I was led a helpless captive, near the southern shore of West Okoboji, is now a favourite summer resort, known as Arnold's Park. Here the trains on the C., M. & St. P. R'y halt, and the steamers on the Okoboji land for the accommodation of tourists.

One mile and a half across the lake on the north shore, on the pre-emption claim of Dr. Harriott, is another popular resort known as Dixon's Beach. Here, where once stood the grimy *teepes* of the Dakotas, may be seen, in summer, the white tents of people of culture and refinement, gleaming amid the dark green foliage of the grand old oaks that spread their branches over this gravelly beach, and crown the picturesque knolls in the background.

The rare beauty of these lakes, as delightful as a bewildering dream of paradise, combined with the purity and brilliancy of the atmosphere, have attracted the attention of capitalists, who have purchased several miles of choice lots on the Okobojis for the purpose of transforming this sylvan country into a fashionable watering-place. But, when the hand of art shall have done its utmost to develop and enhance the charms of nature, it will still be found that the weird traditions of the dusky race that once haunted these shores, and the story of the dark tragedies enacted here, have laid over all a more powerful spell than beauty: the subtle one of romance.

Eighty or one hundred rods southwest of Arnold's Park is what is now called Pillsbury Point. *This* place is the most sacred to me of all on earth. Around it gather life's sweetest and saddest memories. It marks the definite boundary between the bright days of childhood and the darkness and bitterness of the years that have followed. From it radiated the lights and shadows that have fallen across life's pathway. Here stands, in good preservation, the log-house which my father built with his own hands to shelter his family, and around which I have so often played with my little brother. The place is now owned and occupied by Reverend Samuel Pillsbury and the family of his son, (as at time of first publication). These good people have treated me with great kindness and consideration. I am indeed glad this spot, purchased by the blood of my kindred, has fallen into hands so worthy.

No language can express the thrilling emotions that I experienced on my return to this place. It was on a winter's night similar to that one which was so long and dreadful. All the years that had intervened seemed obliterated, and everything appeared the same as in the years long gone. The snow-covered ground, the oak-trees with their seared leaves clinging to their boughs, all seemed the same as on that eventful night. As the shadows darkened I could almost see the dusky forms of the savages filing up to the doorway rifles in hand, crowd into the house, shoot my father when his back was turned, drive mother and sister out of the house, killing them with their guns, tearing the chil-

Mrs. Abbie Gardner Sharp at the Grave.

dren from my arms, and beating them to death with stovewood.

All this, and much more, came involuntarily before me, not as a picture in memory, but as a present reality. The supper-hour having arrived, we gathered around the table. Then the last meal eaten there together by our family rose before me, and so real seemed the vision that I could scarcely control my feelings or swallow a morsel. Having retired to rest the swarthy creatures seemed all about me, murdering, plundering, and ravishing, and I found but little sleep during the night. Again, when the morning dawned, and I heard the prattle of the children of the household, it seemed as though they were the very same whose merry voices were so suddenly changed to dying groans on that fearful night. I could scarcely realize that twenty-seven years, with all their varied experiences, lay between that dreadful night and this morning's waking.

Frequently since then I have visited the place with similar impressions, though perhaps not so vivid. To me this is, and ever must remain, "holy ground," and I cannot but wish it were mine so that I could live here, and die here, and be buried by the side of my kindred. A memorial mound of stones, gathered from the lake shore, has been kindly erected by tourists and strangers, to mark the spot where rest the remains of those most dear to me, which simple recognition I greatly appreciate. A few years ago steps were taken to erect a monument to mark the spot consecrated to civilization by the blood of those early pioneers, but the project, I am sorry to say, was never consummated. I trust it will yet be done by the generous people of Iowa. It is while here on a visit to this sacred spot, seated by the window in the old loghouse, where I can gaze on the mound where lie the ashes of those dearer to me than life, that I bring this volume to a close, and bid the reader farewell.

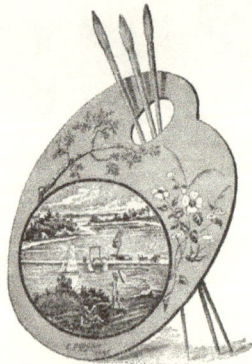

Appendix

TESTIMONIALS

State of Iowa,
Executive Office, Des Moines.
May, 18, 1885.

An examination of the advance sheets of Mrs. Abbie Gardner-Sharp's history and account of the Indian massacre at Spirit Lake convinces me that the work is one of true merit and thrilling interest. It records the most tragic event in the history of the state, and gives young readers a vivid impression not only of the frightful massacre at Spirit Lake, but of the trials and dangers which surrounded the early settlers of Iowa. In my opinion the work is a valuable contribution to the history of the State.

B. R. Sherman,
Governor of Iowa.

Fort Dodge, Iowa, March 2, 1885.

To the Public: Mrs. Sharp has asked me to say briefly what I know concerning the story of her life, and the terrible massacre at Spirit Lake, of which she is one of two survivors. In the fall of 1856 Mr. Angus McBane, Mr. W. W. Marlatt, and myself, made a sort of prospecting tour through North-western Iowa. We reached the Little Sioux river, in the vicinity of the present town of Sioux Rapids, and followed it up to its source in Okoboji Lake. Here we found the first house and family we saw after leaving Fort Dodge. It was the house of Rowland Gardner, the father of Mrs. Sharp. We camped near the house, and for two days explored the lakes and adjacent country. Mrs. Sharp was then a little girl of perhaps thirteen years; bright, cheery, and happy. The next spring Mr. McBane and myself

177

were members of the relief party that, upon report of the massacre, went from Fort Dodge to rescue, if possible, the living, if any should remain, and punish the Indians if they could be overtaken.

Mrs. Sharp tells the story of the massacre and her own sufferings as a captive, and gives the details of her final rescue in the sad and plaintive language of a broken-hearted and noble woman. It is a story of absorbing interest and thrilling pathos. Many of the incidents related are within my personal knowledge. The entire book is part of the history of North western Iowa and South-western Minnesota twenty-eight years ago. It is a record of personal suffering incident to captivity among the Indians, and of the dangers and difficulties of frontier life in other years, which should tend to kindle in the hearts of the present inhabitants of this country a feeling of gratitude to those who pioneered the way to the civilization of these better days. And it is a book that will deeply interest a reader in any part of the country, who loves to read of the pioneer, and to trace the progress of the past; and will especially interest the young and old in North-western Iowa and South-western Minnesota, where it should find a place in every family library.

Very respectfully,

C. C. Carpenter,

Ex-Governor of Iowa,.

I very fully concur with Mr. Carpenter in his statement respecting Mrs. Sharp and her book. I have personal knowledge of many of the incidents of her book, and believe the entire story to be truthful and conscientious.

Angus McBane,

President Merchants National Bank, Ft. Dodge, Iowa.

Chamberlain, Dak., May 4, 1885.

Mrs. Abbie Gardner Sharp, Des Moines, Iowa.

My Dear Lady: Your letter, with proof sheets of several chapters of your forthcoming book, descriptive of the bloody massacre at Spirit Lake, is at hand. From a hasty reading of the chapters before me, I unhestitatingly say it will be a valuable contribution to the earlier history of Iowa and the Northwest.

From a long personal acquaintance with you, and a knowledge of the great worth and respectability of the persons slain by the savages, I am satisfied your narrative is as nearly correct as it is possible for one person to write a history of such an exciting event, after so many years, with their wonderful history, have gone by.

I can most fully and cordially recommend the book as entirely worthy of a place in the Historical Society of Iowa, and of the patronage of the people of the Northwest. I congratulate you on your untiring efforts to accomplish this work, and doubly congratulate you on the success that is now within your easy grasp. I know much of the difficulties you have had to contend with; the ill health, that like a millstone about your neck, would have discouraged and defeated a person with less willpower than you possess.

I hope you may realize full compensation for your labour, and meet with a hearty greeting from your countrymen in this labour of history and recital of facts of the bloodiest drama ever enacted on the rich soil of fair Iowa.

I can only add a devout hope that your last days may be those of rest and comfort, amidst friends and grateful countrymen, as a slight recompense for the sufferings endured in your girlhood days.

With great respect and sympathy,

I am, as ever, your friend,

W. V. Lucas,

Dept. Commander G. A. R. for Dakota.

State of Iowa,

Department of Public Instruction,

Des Moines.

Mrs. Abbie Gardner-Sharp, Des Moines, Iowa.

I have examined with thrilling interest the advance pages of your book, entitled *The History of the Spirit Lake Massacre.*

I must congratulate you, in view of the completeness of the volume and the easy and graceful style in which it is written.

Your book will be a most valuable contribution to the early history of our state, and I am sure, will give to our young readers and to the public generally a truer conception of the perils of pioneer life endured by the brave and true hearted settlers who went before to prepare for the triumph of civilization, the benefits and blessings of which we are enjoying today.

I sincerely hope and believe that your book will soon be found in every household. I most cordially commend your volume to the reading public, in the hope that it may receive the cordial reception which I am sure it deserves.

Very respectfully, your friend,

J. W. Akers,

Supt. Pub. Inst.

5-18-1885.

St. Paul, Minn., Aug. 1, 1885.

Mrs. Abbie Gardner Sharp, Spirit Lake, Iowa.

Dear Madam:—If not too late, I desire to fulfil my promise to send you a prefatory letter to be published with your book entitled *History of the Indian Massacre at Spirit Lake and the Captivity of Abbie Gardner.* Since I saw you I have been a long time away from America and have not been able to comply with your request. I received the Advance proofs of your work and have carefully read them. Their statements are in all things correct as far as my knowledge of the facts and circumstances of the massacre and your captivity and rescue are concerned, and your book is a very interesting contribution to the history of the Northwest.

To the public I will add that at the time of this massacre I was the United States agent for the Sioux of the of the Mississippi stationed at the Sioux agencies on the Redwood and Yellow Medicine Rivers above Fort Ridgeley in the then territory of Minnesota. Ridgeley was the nearest military post to the scene of the massacre and I was the nearest civil officer of the United States Government to that point. The news of the massacre reached the fort and the agencies three or four days after the destruction of the people at Spirit Lake. Colonel Alexander with five companies of the Tenth United States Infantry composed the garrison at the fort.

In consultation we were in doubt at first as to whether the depredations had been committed by my Indians or a roving band of outlaws which frequented the Vermillion and James River valleys, but I soon became convinced that Inkpaduta and his band were responsible for the raid. However, the colonel despatched a company to Spirit Lake which, after a terrible march, and much suffering, arrived there too late to pursue the

Indians, and they with their captives escaped. The territory of Minnesota appropriated $10,000 to compass the rescue of the captives and the whole plan and its execution was by the governor entrusted to me. I succeeded in procuring the liberation of the author of this work; and by these means and the peculiarly advantageous position I occupied for obtaining accurate information concerning the whole affair, I suppose I know as much, if not more about it than any other living man.

Mrs. Sharp spent several months in St. Paul engaged in collecting information for her book, in which labour I gave her all the assistance in my power, and from my records and recollection, furnished her much of the data on which her narrative rests. Of course all the history of her immediate captivity and sufferings is her own. The public can accept the book as perfectly reliable in all its historical facts, and, in my judgment, as an absorbingly interesting narrative of the personal sufferings and experiences of a very worthy member of the band of pioneers who first embarked their fortunes on the then savage border of this now prosperous and happy land.

That your book may meet with a cordial welcome from the public is the wish of your friend.

Chas. E. Flandreau.

It is now six years, (as at time of first publication), since the writer finished the task of sketching the incidents recorded in this volume and presented to the public the *History of the Spirit Lake Massacre*.

The work is now in its third edition—the sale of which were mostly made at the famous Iowa Summer Resort where the scenes of the tragedy transpired.

The author takes pleasure in meeting the tourists who visit the beautiful lake region during the summer months, knowing from thence the work has been carried into nearly every State and Territory in the Union, also in the Dominion of Canada, and into England, where it has been perused with thrilling interest as the many letters received testify.

In conclusion would add to this narrative of personal suffering the testimony of the inestimable good I have received since the publication of the second edition of this volume.

In 1889 my attention was attracted to the "works" of Christian Science, and after these many long years in which I had suffered more than language can express—the result of this terrible experience with the Indians—I was healed by this demonstrable religion.

Christian Science is the key that unlocks the mystery to anyone's satisfaction, who will accept its teachings, the so-called miracles recorded in the Bible.

Science and Health, by Mary Baker G. Eddy, has proven beyond question the revelation of a demonstrable Truth, hence holy (whole) like the body of our Lord and Saviour, and the seamless robe he wore.

Nothing has so appealed to the human mind willing to investigate it, as being the absolute and universal Truth, as this Metaphysical Study, called by its Revelator, Christian Science, for it is all and everything to those who understand.

There is not one burden in life's pathway that may not be lifted, not one sorrow-ladened or sin-burdened creature that may not be helped into the light that lighteth every man in darkness; not one suffering invalid whose pains may not be relieved by its sweet ministry.

Whosoever will, let him take of the waters of life freely.

A. G. S.

* 9 7 8 0 8 5 7 0 6 6 3 8 1 *